FLORIDA CRIME AND JUSTICE

James J. Vardalis, Ph.D.
Debbie Goodman, M.S.

PEARSON

Prentice
Hall

Upper Saddle River, New Jersey 07458

Library of Congress Cataloging-in-Publication Data

Vardalis, James J.
   Florida crime and justice / James J. Vardalis, Debbie Goodman.
      p . cm.
   Includes bibliographical references
   ISBN 0-13-113211-3
  1. Criminal justice, Administration of—Florida. I. Goodman, Debbie
J. II. Title. HV9955.F6 V37 2003 364.9759—dc21

                            2003013206

Editor-in-Chief: Stephen Helba
Director of Production and Manufacturing: Bruce Johnson
Executive Editor: Frank Mortimer, Jr.
Assistant Editor: Sarah Holle
Editorial Assistant: Barbara Rosenberg
Marketing Manager: Tim Peyton
Managing Editor—Production: Mary Carnis
Manufacturing Buyer: Cathleen Petersen
Production Liaison: Denise Brown
Full Service Production: Wendy Druck, The GTS Companies/York, PA Campus
Page Composition: The GTS Companies/York, PA Campus
Design Director: Cheryl Asherman
Design Coordinator: Miguel Ortiz
Cover Design: Carey Davies
Cover Image: GettyImages
Cover Printer: Phoenix Color
Printer/Binder: Banta, Harrisonburg

10 9 8 7 6 5 4 3 2

ISBN 0-13-113211-3

CONTENTS

CHAPTER 3   Crime and Victims in Florida   27

CHAPTER 4   Florida Police Systems   44

CHAPTER 5   Prosecution and Defense   61

CHAPTER 6   The Florida Courts   69

CHAPTER 8   The Florida Correctional System   98

CHAPTER 9   The Florida Juvenile Justice System   110

FOREWORD

After almost 30 years in law enforcement, I can honestly say to those about to enter this profession that no career is more challenging, rewarding, or more important. National contemporary events have created new and unique problems for law enforcement agencies and the entire criminal justice system. New concepts and approaches in the delivery of justice require a thorough understanding of the three components of the system: corrections, the judiciary, and law enforcement. It is abundantly clear that not only must criminal justice professionals be problem solvers, but they must also deploy intelligent strategies contingent upon an analysis of the situation. Knowledge of the entire criminal justice system provides the background necessary to understand the different roles and responsibilities.

Those individuals who are entering this profession will greatly benefit from reading *Florida Crime and Justice*. This textbook presents a comprehensive overview of how all functions within our justice system operate. The book fully explains the interactions among the correctional system, the courts, and law enforcement; chronicles the history of Florida law enforcement, and discusses issues pertaining to crime victims and privatization. Emphasis is on how the three cornerstones of the justice system function, operate, and interact.

By understanding the complexities of all elements within criminal justice, law enforcement trainees will be better equipped to handle the numerous challenges they will be facing. During the past three decades, many positive changes have been made in the Florida justice system that have elevated our profession and made our neighborhoods safer. Dr. James Vardalis and Ms. Debbie Goodman have created an introductory text that should be required reading for all recruits and students of criminal justice.

Carlos Alvarez
Director
Miami–Dade Police Department

ABOUT THE AUTHORS

Dr. James J. Vardalis

Dr. James J. Vardalis has experienced the criminal justice system from both academic and professional positions. Since earning his Master's degree in criminal justice and Ph.D. in public administration from Nova Southern University in Ft. Lauderdale, Florida, he has attended numerous police management schools, including the University of Louisville and the Drug Enforcement Administration National Academy. Dr. Vardalis began his career as a correctional officer in a maximum security state prison assigned to the administration of inmates on death row, and for the next 15 years he served as a police officer. During his full-time law enforcement employment, Dr. Vardalis served in a number of supervisory/command assignments, including patrol, investigations of violent crimes, covert narcotics investigations, and community service programs. He has been state certified as a law enforcement officer in New Jersey, Texas, and Florida. His experience with the judicial system includes over 500 court and grand jury appearances. Additionally, Dr. Vardalis continues to provide consulting for many police agencies throughout the country in areas of promotional assessments, community policing implementation strategies, and police performing studies, and he has published extensively on a variety of justice issues. During his academic career at Florida International University, he taught numerous courses related to understanding crime and the criminal system. Dr. Vardalis is currently a city manager in South Florida.

Debbie Goodman

Ms. Debbie Goodman is the Chairperson of the School of Justice at Miami–Dade Community College. She holds a Master of Science degree in Criminal Justice from Florida International University and a Bachelor of Science degree in Criminology from Florida State University. Ms. Goodman specializes in a wide range of criminal justice topics, including: report writing, ethics, communications, human behavior, juvenile delinquency, criminology, criminal justice, and leadership. She is the author of two national publications, *Report It in Writing* and *Enforcing Ethics,* as well as the originator and series editor of *PACTS: Police and Corrections Training Series.* Ms. Goodman was honored in 2002 by *Who's Who Among America's Teachers* as one of the nation's most talented college instructors. She is committed to providing quality education and training to police and corrections officers, as well as criminal justice students and practitioners. She resides in South Florida with her husband and son.

ACKNOWLEDGMENTS

From James Vardalis

Acknowledgments are difficult due to the immeasurable amount of guidance and assistance one receives when undertaking such an endeavor as researching and writing this book. However, first, my wife, Laura, deserves recognition for her inexhaustible support and assistance.

I would also like to thank Chief Steve Rothlein of the Miami–Dade Police Department; Chief Pete Cuccaro, Miami–Dade School Police; Chief Michael Flint, Florida Department of Law Enforcement; Chief Irving Heller, North Bay Village; Judge Scott Silverman; Maria Ruiz, Esquire; and the city of North Bay Village Mayor Alan Dorne.

Miami–Dade Police Department is among the most professional law enforcement agencies in the state. Director Carlos Alvarez has raised the standards in professionalism, training, and ethics. His insight and direction have been invaluable.

The offices of Katherine Fernandez Rundle, and Joseph Centorino, Esq., State Attorney, Eleventh Judicial Circuit, provided a great deal of information and suggestions.

The contributions of the Performance Improvement Continuum and the Community Crime Prevention Model were provided by Lt. Bernardo Gonzalez, Ed.D, Miami–Dade Police Department, and Ernest G. Vendrell, Ph.D., Lynn University, Boca Raton.

Those involved in the manuscript review, suggestions, and organization are recognized for their patience and professionalism.

I am also indebted to the following agencies: Florida Department of Corrections, Jacksonville Sheriff's Department, Miami–Dade School Police, Broward Sheriff's Department, Monroe Sheriff's Department, Ft. Lauderdale Police Department, Miami–Dade Police Department, Miami Police Department, Miami Beach Police Department, and Florida Department of Law Enforcement.

ACKNOWLEDGMENTS

From Debbie Goodman

To my heroes: Glenn and Connor,
I love you more than words can say.

To Mom and Dad, Corinne and Sam, my family members, and friends,
I am so blessed.

Thank you to Dr. Eduardo Padron, Dr. Jeffrey Lukenbill, Dr. Castell Bryant, Dr. Jose Vicente, Ron Grimming, Mary Greene, Dr. Robert Calabrese, Dr. Donna Jennings, and Chief Thomas Hood at Miami–Dade Community College. I appreciate your support and guidance throughout the years.

Thank you to Robin Baliszewski, Frank Mortimer, Sarah Holle, Barbara Rosenberg, Denise Brown and the dedicated sales representatives at Prentice Hall Publishing.

Thank you to Wendy Druck and all of those involved from The GTS Companies/York, PA Campus.

Thank you to my students for teaching me a great deal about life's lessons.

Thank you to the faculty and staff at Miami–Dade Community College for being wonderful people to work with especially Anna Leggett, Ed Hargis, Miriam Lorenzo, Clyde Pfleegor, Sam Latimore, Wiley Huff, Mike Grimes, Clark Zen, Amarilys Ramos, Julie Lamelas, and Merelyn Benedetto.

A special thanks to Florida's police and correction officers for your exemplary service to our communities. May you lead long, happy, and healthy lives.

CHAPTER 1

The Development of Police in Florida

CHAPTER OVERVIEW

This chapter provides an overview of the development of Florida, demographic and population shifts, and the growth of its cities. Also, the railroad industry, law enforcement evolution and problems, and the history of the Florida County Sheriff are discussed. Other issues addressed center around contemporary policing, with a look to the future and the direction of law enforcement in Florida.

THE HISTORY OF FLORIDA LAW ENFORCEMENT

Not until the mid-1800s did law enforcement begin to shift from community volunteers to a more organized system with compensation benefits. The history of Florida in terms of organized law enforcement begins during the national reconstruction period after the Civil War. Understanding the historical development of Florida and its law enforcement roots is important to the examination of modern policing. The study of the past provides insight and understanding regarding many of the current practices of and perceptions about police.

Early in the 1800s, Florida was, for the most part, an undeveloped area of land with few residents. In 1845, a population census of Dade County reported 314 people: 263 white, 29 slaves, and 22 free blacks. Monroe County reported 618 people: 452 white, 93 slaves, and 73 free blacks. Florida Indians were not considered in the population count. On March 3, 1845, President Tyler signed the necessary documents making Florida a state (Tebeau, 1971).

Florida entered the Union as a slave state with a population of about 140,000 people, of whom 63,000 were black. On January 10, 1861, Florida voted 62 to 7 to secede from the Union. In addition to the 15,000 confederate soldiers, Florida also contributed cattle from mid-state areas and salt from St. Andrews Bay (Panama City). Jacksonville served as a pawn during the conflict, with the city falling to federal troops in March of 1863. The civil conflict, which ended by surrender in Tallahassee on May 10, 1865, had a profound impact on the growth of Florida. Confederate soldiers were released rapidly and many made their way to Florida. Additionally, many business people from the north saw opportunity in the economic depressed postwar land of Florida. Henry A. DeLand, General Henry S. Sanford, and John B. Stetson were significant northern contributors to the growth of Florida (Tebeau, 1971).

Military Law Enforcement

As part of the reconstruction of the south, on March 2, 1867, Congress passed the Military Bill, which divided the south into five districts. Florida, Alabama, and Georgia were contained within the third district. Under military law, the southern states were to write new constitutions, grant universal suffrage to all males over 21 years of age, and ratify the 14th Amendment (Cox and Dovell, 1974).

Early Law Enforcement Problems

By 1868–1870, Florida was experiencing an outbreak of violence and lawlessness. The Ku Klux Klan committee of Congress reported 256 pages of testimony of witnesses regarding 55 acts of murder and violence in Florida alone. The population was growing; in 1880, Florida had a population of 269,493. The diverse population included soldiers from both the north and south, political reformers, opportunists, business investors, and common criminals, as well as families seeking better lives who provided ample crime victims. This was also a period of rapid growth for Florida. Numerous deposits of phosphate were discovered, railroads were beginning to advance deeper south, innumerable citrus groves were planted, and swampland was converted into farmland (Tebeau, 1971).

On January 10, 1877, Governor Drew urged a reduction of costs for the State of Florida. He focused on the state penitentiary system, which had an average annual budget of $25,000. He suggested to the legislature that this excessive cost could be offset by allowing the governor "to hire out the prisoners upon conditions as may be deemed most advantageous to the state" (Tebeau, 1971).

CITY GROWTH IN THE LATE 1800s

In the late 1800s, Jacksonville was the most populated city, with 25,130; followed by Key West, 16,502; Tampa, 15,634; Pensacola, 14,084; Ocala, 4567; St. Augustine, 4151; Tallahassee, 3931; and Apalachicola, 3061. The rank order of other cities by population was Fernandina, Orlando, Palatka, Lake City, Bartow, Milton, DeLand, Sanford, Daytona, Jasper, Kissimmee, and West Palm Beach. Almost all who traveled through Florida utilized the waterways. In terms of counties, the 1870 federal census indicated that Alachua was the most populated, with 17,328; Leon County was second, with 15,236; followed by Jefferson, 13,398; Duval, 11,921; Madison, 11,121; and Marion, 10,804 (Tebeau, 1971).

THE RAILROAD INDUSTRY

Henry M. Flagler was a partner of John D. Rockefeller in the Standard Oil Company. When he moved to Florida in 1878, Flagler had an interest in developing a better railroad system for the state. In 1883, he secured a charter for a railroad line into the southern frontier of Miami.

Along with transportation into southern Florida, he also provided luxury tourist hotels, such as the Breakers in Palm Beach and the Royal Palm Hotel in Miami. Flagler was one of the most significant contributors to the development and population expansion of South Florida.

GOVERNORS OF FLORIDA

Governor	Years Served	Governor	Years Served
William D. Moseley	1845–1849	Francis P. Fleming	1889–1893
Thomas Brown	1849–1853	Henry L. Mitchell	1893–1897
James E. Broome	1853–1857	William D. Bloxham	1897–1901
Madison Perry	1857–1861	William Jennings	1901–1905
John Milton	1861–1865	Napoleon B. Broward	1905–1909
Abraham K. Allison	—[a]	Albert W. Gilchrist	1909–1913
William Marvin (provisional)	1865	Park Trammell	1913–1917
David Shelby Walker	1866–1868	Sidney I. Catts	1917–1921
Harrison Reed	1868–1873	Cary A. Hardee	1921–1925
Ossian B. Hart	1873–1874	John W. Martin	1925–1929
Marcellus L. Stearns	1874–1877	Doyle F. Carlton	1929–1933
George F. Drew	1877–1881	David Sholtz	1933–1937
William D. Bloxham	1881–1885	Fred P. Cone	1937–1941
Edward A. Perry	1885–1889	Spessard L. Holland	1941–1945

Governor	Years Served	Governor	Years Served
Millard Caldwell	1945–1949	Claude R. Kirk, Jr.	1967–1971
Fuller Warren	1949–1953	Reubin Askew	1971–1979
Daniel T. McCarty	1953–1953	Bob Graham	1979–1987
Charley E. Johns	1953–1955	Robert Martinez	1987–1991
LeRoy Collins	1955–1961	Lawton Chiles	1991–1998[b]
C. Farris Bryant	1961–1965	Buddy MacKay	1998 (3 weeks)
W. Haydon Burns	1965–1967	Jeb Bush	1999–present

[a]Allison, as president of the Senate, assumed governorship upon the suicide death of John Milton; however, this transition took place under the confederacy and was not recognized by the new Union government (Tebeau, 1971).
[b]Chiles died December 13, 1998, three weeks before leaving office. Lt. Govenor MacKay completed the term.

CONTEMPORARY FLORIDA GOVERNMENT

Today, Florida still operates under some aspects of the 1885 constitution, with revisions in 1968 and certain later amendments. The governor is the chief executive and is elected to a 4-year term (not to exceed 10 consecutive years). The state legislative branch contains the Senate, comprised of 40 members who serve 4-year terms, and the House of Representatives, which has 120 members who serve 2-year terms.

About the State of Florida

Total land area: 58,664 square miles

Capital: Tallahassee

Largest city in population: Jacksonville 672,971 (1990)

Number of counties: 67

Total population: 13,600,000 (2000)

Density: 238.9 persons per square mile

Distribution: 90.8% metropolitan, 9.2% rural

Per capita income: $16,546

Electoral college votes: 21

Nickname: The Sunshine State

THE EARLY FLORIDA COUNTY SHERIFF

The concept of sheriff and constable originated in England and was transported with the early American colonists. In the 1800s, most communities had a sheriff to provide peace and order. The duties of the sheriffs were similar to those of their English counterparts (Walker, 1992). The sheriffs in most areas, prior to 1900, were appointed by the governor. The layout of counties in Florida in the early 1800s was somewhat different than today. When Dade County was established in 1836, the land area at that time included what is now Miami–Dade, Broward, Palm Beach, and Martin Counties. Juno was the county seat for Dade from 1836 until 1899, when the seat was moved to Miami. Palm Beach County became an independent county in 1909, and other counties were formed, divided, and consolidated as the population grew and shifted. As counties began to recognize growing law enforcement needs, they created sheriff's offices. Leon County formed its sheriff's office in 1842, and others soon followed.

GROWTH AND LAW ENFORCEMENT PROBLEMS IN FLORIDA

In the 1800s, the sheriff's office was the principal method of law enforcement. Napoleon Broward was appointed sheriff of Duval County in 1888, was elected to that position in 1892, and became governor in 1902. The convict lease system ended in 1923 in Leon County, after a North Dakota youth died under circumstances that pointed to abuse. This long-standing practice of leasing out prisoners was initiated by Governor Drew in 1878. The system involved private employers leasing convicts for labor. The employers would feed and clothe each prisoner and pay an annual fee to the state.

In the 1940s, gambling and off-track betting began to emerge as potential threats to state revenue, subsequently becoming a serious law enforcement issue. An anti-bookie bill was passed by the legislature. In 1950, the Miami Crime Commission, investigated Governor Fuller Warren, who was a one-time member of the Ku Klux Klan (Tebeau, 1971). Several law enforcement officials were under indictment, but Governor Warren refused to remove all but Sheriff Walter Clark, who admitted having part ownership of a gambling house. In October of 1950, a Miami–Dade County grand jury indicted Sheriff Jimmy Sullivan on evidence submitted by the Kefauver Crime Investigations Committee of the U.S. Senate, the Miami Crime Commission, and the *Miami Herald*. The indictment was later overturned by the Supreme Court. During the 1950s, Florida established a reputation of corruption and organized gambling protected by public officials and police. Compounding this problem were bombings throughout Florida in synagogues and black-owned businesses and homes.

POPULATION CHANGES

Governmental changes in Cuba had a significant impact on South Florida. When Fidel Castro assumed control over Cuba in 1960, approximately 11,000 Cubans fled to Miami. In 1961, during a short lift of the immigration ban, thousands of people fled Cuba. Two flights every day ultimately accounted for approximately 182,375 new residents. By 1970, Cubans were fleeing their country for Miami at a rate of 2800 per month. It is estimated that more than 364,000 registered with the Cuban refugee program in Miami. Not all refugees registered and some relocated; however, a great majority contributed to the rapid Miami–Dade County growth (Tebeau, 1971). The population of Florida almost doubled from 1960 to 1980. The 1990 census reported permanent residents of Florida at 12,937,926, up 32.7% over the previous decade. The top five cities in order of population in 1990 were Jacksonville, Miami, Tampa, Fort Lauderdale, and Hialeah.

MORE PROBLEMS FOR THE RAPID GROWTH OF SOUTH FLORIDA

The 1980 police beating of Arthur McDuffie and subsequent Miami police coverup of the facts in this incident led to a major riot in Dade County (Porter and Dunn, 1984). The civil unrest invoked an inquiry by the U.S. Commission on Civil Rights. Another incident of national interest erupted in 1985, when Miami police officers attempted to rip off drug smugglers on the vessel *Mary C,* docked along the Miami River. Three people from the boat jumped into the dark river and drowned. The subsequent federal investigation resulted in about 90 police officers being arrested, fired, suspended, or reprimanded (Dunham and Alpert, 1993). This case is commonly referred to as the "Miami River Cops" case.

MIAMI–DADE COUNTY

As circumstances contributed to urban growth of some areas, municipal police departments emerged. Today, law enforcement is the largest component within the state criminal justice system. The state is divided into 67 counties, each having its own county sheriff's office, with the exception of Miami–Dade County, which adopted a metropolitan form of government in 1957, at which time the Miami–Dade County sheriff's office was changed to the Public Safety Department. The county at that time had a population of approximately 500,000 people and covered approximately 2139 square miles. In 1960, 623 additional officers were added in conjunction with the policing responsibilities for the Port of Miami and Miami International Airport. In 1966, controversy over appointing or electing the Dade County sheriff was resolved by voter mandate. A non-elected Dade County sheriff method was implemented in which the County Manager would appoint the Director of the Public Safety Department and Sheriff of Metropolitan Dade County. The Miami–Dade County Public Safety Department was required to provide a vast array of services, including fire protection, corrections, management of the county jail and the county stockade, civil defense, animal control, motor vehicle inspections, and county police and investigation functions.

By 1973, most of the non-police-related duties had been divested into other county departments, and the 1200 sworn personnel devoted their efforts to police services. In 1981, they were reorganized and emerged as the Metro-Dade Police Department (MDPD). The current 2800 police officers are supported by 1200 civilian employees and represent the largest police department in the southeastern United States. Miami–Dade County also contains 26 separate municipal police departments (see Chapter 2).

DUVAL COUNTY

The City of Jacksonville was mapped out in 1822 and named after the first territorial governor, Andrew Jackson. The St. Johns River made Jacksonville the leading deep water port in the southeastern United States. Dramatically different from Miami–Dade County, Duval County contains one police agency. Prior to August, 1967, each municipality maintained its own police agency and city government, but a citizen vote to consolidate all governmental bodies and agencies changed the method of police service delivery. On October 1, 1968, the Office of the Sheriff–Jacksonville Police Department emerged as the sole agency responsible for police service. The 1990 census reported the population as 672,971 with a land area of 776 square miles. The 1400 police officers provide countywide law enforcement, except for the jurisdictions of Atlantic Beach, Jacksonville Beach, and Neptune Beach.

CONTEMPORARY POLICING IN FLORIDA

The migration of people to Florida has been dramatic. In 1880, the total state population reached 269,000, double the count of 1870. Concern surrounding the growth of the state population necessitated the establishment of a Commissioner of Immigration as one of the offices of the governor's cabinet (Cox and Dovell, 1974). Today's estimated 13,000,000 permanent Florida residents are compounded by the 36,000,000 visitors each year (Florida Division of Tourism, 1990). The police industry in Florida has attempted to keep pace with the inflating population. The 341 law enforcement agencies employ almost 34,000 sworn personnel (see Chapter 2). The *Uniform Crime Report* (FBI, 1994) indicates that Florida experienced 569 murders, 3412 forcible rapes, 23,756 robberies, 47,179 aggravated assaults, 120,000 burglaries, 290,000 larcenies, and 53,000 vehicle thefts (FDLE, 1994).

Police Women in Florida

While early law enforcement in Florida ignored women, this practice appears to be diminishing. Women and minorities are having an impact on the makeup of police organizations throughout the country. The Metropolitan Police Department in the District of Columbia indicated in a 1972 study that women can perform police patrol work as well as men. In fact, the study suggested that women may be less aggressive and less likely than men to engage in serious unbecoming conduct. These may be important traits in light of the introduction of community policing (FDLE, 1994). The 1993 Florida Department of Law Enforcement report indicated that women make up about 11% of all Florida law enforcement officers.

	Male	**Female**
State law enforcement	2573	259
County and local	29,158	3500

Outlook for the Police

Years of growth have taken a toll on Florida. Development of cities has produced increased crime and disorder. Many areas of Florida law enforcement are experiencing financial pressures due to the increases in population, complexity of crime investigations, and rising costs. Such crimes as computer crimes, sophisticated drug trafficking organizations, economic crimes (such as credit card fraud, identity theft, household repair scams, and retail theft), and child abuse are compounded by information delivery systems that enhance public awareness and lead to unreasonable demands. Serious problems exist for law enforcement. Attempts to deliver traditional police service clash with fewer available resources. Suggestions have been made to revamp the 150-year-old traditional role of policing and to examine different approaches of protecting the public. New styles of policing are intriguing, and potential police and community leaders, as well as students of criminal justice, can influence such changes.

CONCLUSION

It was not until the mid 1800s that Florida law enforcement shifted from community volunteers to a more organized system with compensation benefits. Problems faced by Florida in development of its law enforcement system included issues involving the Ku Klux Klan, population and city growth, railroad construction, and tourism. Prior to 1960, South Florida consisted of several small southern military towns. The massive immigration into South Florida commencing in the early 1960s transformed small communities into multicultural metropolitan areas. Contemporary policing must address issues encompassing community policing, women among the ranks of Florida police forces, rising crime rates, financial pressures, computer crimes, drug and child abuse, and political corruption.

At a Glance: The 67 Counties in Florida

Alachua County was established in 1824 from a portion of St. Johns County and named for a Spanish ranch existing in the vicinity in 1680. Two derivations have been proposed for the name: *la* ("the" in Spanish), *chua* ("sink" in Seminole), and *luchuwa* ("jug" in Seminole). The name is thought to refer to a large chasm 2.5 miles southeast of Gainesville.

Baker County was established in 1861 from New River County and named for James McNair Baker (1822–1992), Confederate States senator and judge in Florida's Fourth Judicial District. The Civil War Battle of Olustee was fought just east of the town of Olustee.

Bay County was established from Washington County in 1913 and named for St. Andrew's Bay, which borders the county. During World War II, Panama City developed as a shipbuilding and industrial center.

Bradford County was established as New River County in 1858 from portions of Columbia and Alachua counties. It was renamed in 1861 in honor of Captain Richard Bradford, the first Florida officer killed in the Civil War.

Brevard County was established in 1844 from a portion of Mosquito County and was originally named St. Lucie. In 1855, the name was changed in honor of Theodore Washington Brevard (1804–1877) of North Carolina. Brevard came to Florida in 1847 and became the state comptroller.

Broward County was established in 1915 from a portion of Miami–Dade County and named for Napoleon B. Broward, governor from 1905 to 1909 and a principal proponent of early efforts to drain the Everglades.

Calhoun County was established from a portion of Escambia County in 1838. The county was named for John C. Calhoun, Senator from South Carolina and an outspoken advocate of the doctrine of states' rights.

Charlotte County was established in 1921 from a portion of De Soto County and named for Charlotte Harbor. "Charlotte" may be a corruption of *Carlos* or *Calos*, words associated with the Calusa, the Indian group in southwest Florida at the time of Spanish contact. During the 1970s, Charlotte County became one of Florida's fastest growing counties.

Citrus County was established in 1887 from Hernando County and named in honor of the citrus fruit. The Crystal River Indian mounds and museum are in Citrus County. David Levy Yulee, U.S. Senator from Florida, established a thriving sugar plantation and mill near the town of Homosassa. The Yulee mansion was burned by Union troops in 1864 and the mill left in ruins.

Clay County was established in 1858 from a portion of Duval County and named for Kentuckian Henry Clay, Secretary of State under John Quincy Adams. In the late 1800s, the St. Johns River and Green Cove Springs were popular tourist spots.

Collier County was established from a portion of Lee County in 1923 and named for advertising tycoon Barron G. Collier, one of South Florida's leading developers.

Columbia County was established in 1832 from St. Johns County and was named in honor of Christopher Columbus. The Spanish explorer Hernando De Soto founded a large village on the site of present-day Lake City.

De Soto County was established from a portion of Manatee County in 1887 and named for Spanish explorer Hernando de Soto.

Dixie County was established from Lafayette County in 1921 and named for the nickname of the South. Andrew Jackson defeated Seminole Chief Billy Bowlegs at Old Town in Dixie County.

Duval County was established in 1822 from St. Johns County and was named for William Pope Duval, first territorial governor of Florida. Jacksonville was nearly destroyed by fire in 1901. One of the largest ports in the state, Jacksonville developed a substantial shipbuilding industry during World War II.

Escambia County, named for the Escambia River, was established in 1821 and was one of the first two counties in Florida. The derivation of "Escambia" is unclear, although it is probably of Indian origin. Tristan de Luna established a settlement at present-day Pensacola in 1559.

Flagler County was established in 1917 from portions of St. Johns and Volusia counties and named for Henry Morrison Flagler, developer of the Florida East Coast Railroad.

Franklin County was established from a portion of Escambia County in 1832 and named for Benjamin Franklin. Spanish explorer Panfilo de Narvaez visited the area near present-day Apalachicola in 1527. In 1845, Dr. John Gorrie of Apalachicola built the first ice-making machine.

Gadsden County was established in 1823 and named for James Gadsden (1788–1858), native of South Carolina and aide-de-camp to Andrew Jackson during his 1818 campaign in Florida. The county was settled by slave owners from other southern states and became famous for its tobacco.

Gilchrist County was the last county formed in Florida. In 1925, it was established from a portion of Alachua County and named for Albert Waller Gilchrist, the state's 20th governor (1909–1913).

Glades County was established from De Soto County in 1921 and named for the Everglades.

Gulf County was established in 1925 from a portion of Calhoun County and named for the Gulf of Mexico. Port St. Joe (first called St. Joseph) was one of the first towns established on the Gulf and was the terminus of the Lake Wimico and St. Joseph Canal Railroad, one of the first three steam-engine railroads built in the United States. In 1838, the first state constitutional convention was held in St. Joseph near present-day Port St. Joe.

Hamilton County was established from a portion of Escambia County in 1827 and named for Alexander Hamilton, first U.S. Secretary of the Treasury. The Florida Folklife Program is housed at the Stephen Foster Memorial in White Springs, where each year in May the Florida Folk Festival is held.

Hardee County was established in 1921 from a portion of De Soto county and named for Cary Augustus Hardee, who was governor the year the county was formed. Wauchula was the site of a military post built during the Seminole Wars.

(continued)

Hendry County was established in 1923 from a portion of Lee County and named for Captain Francis Asbury Hendry, an early settler and the "cattle king" of South Florida.

Herando County was named for the Spanish explorer Hernando de Soto and was established in 1843 from pieces of Hillsborough, Mosquito, and Alachua counties. The name was changed to Benton in honor of Thomas Hart Benton in 1844, but was restored to Hernando in 1850.

Highlands County was established from a portion of De Soto County in 1921 and named for its rolling countryside.

Hillsborough County was established in 1834 from St. Johns County and named for Wills Hills, the Earl of Hillsborough.

Holmes County was established in 1848 from portions of Walton and Jackson counties and named for Holmes Creek, the county's eastern boundary. The name "Holmes" is thought to be either from an Indian chieftain with the given name Holmes or from Thomas J. Holmes, a settler from North Carolina.

Indian River County was established in 1925 from a portion of St. Lucie County and named for the Indian River.

Jackson County was established from Escambia County in 1822 and named for Andrew Jackson, governor of the territories of East and West Florida and later president of the United States. Marianna was the site of a battle in 1864, during which old men and young boys fought against the invasion of federal forces.

Jefferson County was established in 1827 from Escambia County and named for President Thomas Jefferson, who died in 1826. Before the Civil War, Jefferson County had developed into a plantation-based agriculture society. Many houses from that era remain in Monticello, the county seat.

Lafayette County was established from a portion of Madison County in 1856 and named for the Marquis de Lafayette (1757–1834), who was given a township in the Tallahassee area but never visited the state.

Lake County was established in 1887 from portions of Sumter and Orange counties and named for its large number of lakes.

Lee County was established from Monroe County in 1823 and named for General Robert E. Lee.

Leon County was established from a portion of Escambia County in 1824 and named for the Spanish explorer, Juan Ponce de Leon. On the second voyage of Columbus, Ponce de Leon sighted Florida in the spring of 1513 and named the land "Pascua Florida," after the Feast of Flowers being held at that time. Present-day Leon County was the center of the Apalachee Indian culture when Hernando de Soto arrived in 1539.

Levy County was established in 1845 from a portion of Alachua County and named for David Levy Yulee, first U.S. Senator from Florida and developer of a 5000-acre plantation on the Homosassa River. Cedar Key was founded in 1850 and was the southern terminus of the first railroad across Florida.

Liberty County was established from Gadsden County in 1855 and named for the concept of liberty.

Madison County was established in 1827 from a portion of Escambia County and named for President James Madison.

Manatee County was established in 1855 from portions of Hillsborough and Mosquito counties. The county was named for the manatees (also known as the sea cows) found in its waters. According to some accounts, Hernando de Soto landed on Terra Ceia Island and began his trek north from present-day Manatee County.

Marion County was established from portions of Alachua and Mosquito counties in 1844 and named for General Francis Marion, the "Swamp Fox" of the Revolutionary War.

Martin County was established in 1925 from a portion of Palm Beach County and from a much smaller portion of St. Lucie County. The county was named for John W. Martin, governor from 1925 to 1929.

Miami–Dade County was established in 1836 from a portion of St. Johns County and named for Major Francis Longhorne Miami–Dade, U.S. Army Commander during the Second Seminole War.

Monroe County was established in 1823 from a portion of St. Johns County and named for President James Monroe, fifth president of the United States. In 1513, Spanish explorer Juan Ponce de Leon sailed past the keys. For the next three centuries, the keys became a haven for pirates and adventurers. Many English-speaking settlers came to the keys from the Grand Bahamas, and by 1821, when the United States acquired Florida, Key West was the state's most populous city.

Nassau County was established from St. Johns County in 1824 and named for Nassau Sound, which separates Nassau and Duval counties. The name comes from the capital of the Bahamas, which was named for the Duchy of Nassau, a former German state.

Oceola County was established in 1887 from portions of Orange and Brevard counties and named for Osceola, leader of the Seminoles who was captured and imprisoned by General Thomas S. Jesup under a flag of truce.

Okaloosa County was established in 1915 from portions of Santa Rosa and Walton counties. "Okaloosa" is possibly derived from Choctaw *aka* for "water" and *lusa* for "black." The combination of these two words may refer to the Blackwater River in Okaloosa County.

Okeechobee County was established from portions of Osceola and Brevard counties in 1917. The name is derived from two Hitchiti words: *Oki* for "water" and *Chobi* for "big."

Orange County was established in 1824 from a portion of St. Johns County. Originally named Mosquito, the county was renamed Orange in 1845 for the many orange groves in the area.

Palm Beach County was established in 1909 from a portion of Miami–Dade County and named for the coconut palms that lined the Atlantic Ocean beaches.

Pasco County was established in 1887 from a portion of Hernando County and named for Samuel Pasco of Monticello, speaker of the Florida House of Representatives at the time the county was created and later a U.S. senator.

Pinellas County was established in 1911 from a portion of Hillsborough County. The name is derived from the Spanish *Punto Pinal,* meaning "point of pines."

Polk County was established in 1861 from portions of Brevard and Hillsborough counties and named for James Knox Polk, 11th president of the United States.

Putnam County was established from St. Johns and Alachua counties in 1849 and named for Benjamin Alexander Putnam (1801–1869), lawyer, soldier, judge, member of the state legislature, and first president of the Florida Historical Society.

Santa Rosa County was established in 1842 from a portion of Escambia County and named for Santa Rosa Island, which was named for the Catholic saint Rosa de Viterbo.

Sarasota County was established in 1921 from a portion of Manatee County. The exact meaning of the name is unknown and may be of Indian origin. The name was first applied to a prominent part of the county's shoreline known as Point O' Rocks. Early versions of the name include "Sarasote," "Sarazota," and "Sara Zota."

Seminole County was established from Orange County in 1913 and named for the Seminole Indians. Seminole is thought to be derived from the Spanish *cimarron,* meaning "wild" or "runaway."

St. Johns County was established in 1821 as one of Florida's original two counties, the other being Escambia. The county was named for the St. Johns River. In 1565, Pedro Menendez de Aviles founded a settlement at St. Augustine. The town, continuously settled since that time, and the nearby Castillo de San Marcos attract thousands of visitors each year.

(continued)

St. Lucie County was established from a portion of Mosquito County in 1844 and named for St. Lucie of Syracuse. The name was changed to Brevard during the 1850s, but in 1905 the original name of St. Lucie was restored.

Sumter County was established from a portion of Mosquito County in 1853 and named for General Thomas Sumter (1736–1832), a South Carolinian prominent in the Revolutionary War.

Suwannee County was established from Columbia County in 1858 and named for the Suwannee River, immortalized by Stephen Foster's song, "Way Down Upon the Swanee River." Considerable disagreement exists over the origin of the name. Two possibilities are the Cherokee word *Sawani*, meaning "echo river," and corruption of Spanish *San Juan*.

Taylor County was established from a portion of Madison County in 1856 and named for Zachary Taylor, Commander of federal forces during the Second Seminole War and 12th president of the United States.

Union County was established from a portion of Bradford County in 1921. The county was to be named New River, the original name of Bradford County. The source of the name Union is unclear, although it has been suggested that Union resulted from the fact that both parts of Bradford County were united in desiring a separation.

Volusia County was established from a portion of Mosquito County in 1854 and named for a landing called *Volusia* near Lake George on the St. Johns River. The origin of the name is unknown but may be from a Frenchman or Belgian named *Veluche*.

Wakulla County was established from a portion of Leon County in 1843. "Wakulla," also the name of an enormous spring and river in the county, is probably of Indian derivation. It may contain the word *kala*, meaning "spring of water" in some Indian dialects, or *wahkola*, meaning "loon" in Hitchiti, a language of the Creek Indians.

Walton County was established in 1824 from a portion of Escambia County and named for Col. George Walton, secretary of the Territory of West Florida (1821–1822) and of the combined territory of Florida (1822–1826).

Washington County was established from a portion of Escambia County in 1825 and named for George Washington, first U.S. president.

DISCUSSION QUESTIONS

1. What was the status of Florida during the Civil War?

2. When did Florida enter the Union?

3. Discuss growth development during the late 1800s.

4. How did immigration from Cuba affect law enforcement in Florida?

5. Why is Duval County unique in its law enforcement structure?

REFERENCES

Cox, M. G. and J. E. Dovell. 1974. *Florida from Secession to Space Age.* St. Petersburg, Fla.: Great Outdoors Publishing House.

Dunham, R. G. and G. P. Alpert. 1993. *Critical Issues in Policing: Contemporary Readings.* Prospect Heights, Ill.: Waveland Press.

Federal Bureau of Investigation (FBI). 1994. *Crime in the United States: Uniform Crime Reports 1994.* Washington, D.C.: Federal Bureau of Investigation.

Florida Department of Banking and Finance (FDBF). 1989. *State of Florida Local Government Financial Report: Fiscal Year 1988–1989.* Tallahassee, Fla.: Florida Department of Banking and Finance.

Florida Department of Commerce (FDC). 1989. *Florida County Comparisons.* Tallahassee, Fla.: Florida Department of Commerce.

Florida Department of Law Enforcement (FDLE). 1994. *Crime in Florida.* Tallahassee, Fla.: Florida Department of Law Enforcement.

Florida Division of Tourism. 1990. *Florida Tourist Study: An Executive Summary.* Tallahassee, Fla.

Porter, B. and M. Dunn. 1984. *The Miami Riot of 1980.* Lexington, Mass: Lexington Books.

Tebeau, C. W. 1971. *A History of Florida.* Coral Gables, Fla: University of Miami Press.

Walker, S. 1992. *The Police in America: An Introduction.* New York: McGraw-Hill.

CHAPTER 2

Community Policing in Florida

CHAPTER OVERVIEW

This chapter reviews community policing in Florida, including its problems and prospects. The models associated with policing are discussed in depth, as is a comparison of traditional policing and community policing. We exam the development of American police systems, the reputation of police, fiscal resources, jails and prisons, and eras of policing in Florida.

COMMUNITY POLICING IN FLORIDA: PROBLEMS AND PROSPECTS

In many communities throughout Florida, a quiet revolution in the nature of policing is taking place. In these communities, an approach termed *community policing* (see Appendix 1) is being implemented (Kelling, 1988). Community policing conveys the idea that departments are returning to the earlier era of the "neighborhood cop." In some areas, police officers are out of their cars, walking beats, with little else changing in terms of how they carry out their duties. In other areas, the changes are much more significant, and communities are working with their community police officers in ways that were unimaginable 5 years ago.

THE PROFESSIONAL MODEL

The emergence of community policing has been an outgrowth of the recognition that the professional police model has been unsuccessful in controlling crime problems that confront most communities and of the feeling that law-abiding citizens have little contact with their police. In some of these communities, such as Delray Beach, where extensive surveys have been conducted, the fear of crime was significantly affecting the quality of life in the community, as citizens no longer felt safe in their houses and in the community. In more deteriorated areas, street sales of drugs, the presence of gangs, and spreading urban decay led to a call to do something different (Wiatrowski, 1995).

The prospects of being able to control crime through policing, arrest, and other deterrence-based strategies are neither optimistic nor based on research. Florida has one of the highest crime rates in the country according to official statistics (FBI, 1990). These statistics are somewhat misleading because only about one-third of the crimes committed are reported to the police. The influx of persons from other countries taking up residence in Florida over the past 25 years has included new and illegal immigrants who are much less willing to report their victimization to the police. They either fear the behavior of the police due to their experiences in the countries they fled or fear being deported. Furthermore, the police close about 20% of all reported crimes, but actually only about 7% of the crimes are solved.

FISCAL RESOURCES

Fiscal constraints make it unlikely that significant additional resources will be devoted to increasing the number of police officers in communities. In fact, some relatively small communities, such as Pompano Beach, have lost almost 25% of their police force over the past 5 years due to declining tax bases. Annually, police departments struggle to defend the number of officers they have in the face of competing demands for a limited budget, despite the cries of politicians that crime is rising.

JAILS AND PRISONS

In the past 10 years, the number of prison spaces in the United States has doubled, resulting in one of the highest incarceration rates in the world. In the United States, almost 271 individuals are incarcerated per 100,000 population. In Florida, the rate of incarceration of 307 per 100,000 exceeds the national averages. The crushing cost of these policies has caused some states to be unable to pay for other municipal services and education. Furthermore, proposals for "three strikes and you're out" are projected to make it impossible for some states, such as California, to expand their university system (Rand Corporation, 1994). While most argue that violent and repeat offenders should be incarcerated, it is clear that the criminal justice system is not an acceptable fix for the breakdown of many American institutions and communities. Clearly, it is time to explore some alternatives to this situation.

THE DEVELOPMENT OF AMERICAN POLICE SYSTEMS

Examination of the history of American law enforcement reveals that at least three distinctive eras can be identified. The development of law enforcement in the United States is an outgrowth of two divergent trends. First, the geographical distances that separate population areas have resulted in a strong tradition of local autonomy in law enforcement. Second, by the 1840s, the impact of urbanization had resulted in traditional methods of social control such as sheriffs and night watchmen becoming ineffective. The result was that, by the mid-19th century, most of the larger cities in the northeast were experimenting with the development of police forces; however, because of the geographical distances, these departments developed independently from each other. In Florida, what are now the largest cities had populations of less than 1000, and many towns were only small settlements along the coast having only one or two police officers. In contrast, England, which began developing its police force somewhat earlier, is smaller geographically and organizationally and is more centralized. The idea of a police officer on the beat being responsible for the residents of an area was more firmly fixed in England, and the officers were less likely to abuse their police powers.

Also at this time, the American political system was evolving. By the 1850s, much of America was heavily involved in partisan politics. Political parties controlled many of the activities of local and national governments. Political parties were well organized at the local level and brought the benefits of government to their local constituents. The "spoils system" resulted in patronage being directed to those loyal to the party.

In this era, the police were part of the system and many examples can be cited of police departments being corrupted by participation in this system. The police function in this era was broadly defined and decentralized because of the lack of communications. The officer went to his beat in the morning and worked throughout the area. The officer's knowledge of the area and its residents was immense. The officers were largely autonomous, with little direct supervision from their superiors. The police were broadly responsible for what is now termed "order maintenance." Specifically, the police controlled disorderly and unruly elements in the community, such as vagrants, prostitutes, alcoholics, and petty criminals. Those who violated community standards were either forced to comply or encouraged to leave. Police officers also participated in a wide range of activities that contributed to the quality of life in the community. Jails were open in the winter so that homeless persons could sleep in them. Food was provided for the hungry, and jobs were located for those who needed employment. While police responded to the crime problem in the community, they were not solely responsible for dealing with it.

Unfortunately, in this era some aspects of policing were less than satisfactory. The use of violence or brutality not specifically authorized by the law to maintain order was common. Racial and ethnic minorities, as well as those economically disadvantaged, were encouraged to leave an area with the aid of a nightstick and the tacit support of the public when it was thought that they did not fit into the community. Thus, when the achievement of order became a goal by itself, without examination of the means by which it was achieved, the questionable use of force became common. The police also enforced segregation and did not protect minorities from racial violence. During lynchings, the police would either disappear or stand to the side of the mob.

THE REPUTATION OF POLICE

The police generally experienced a poor reputation, and Florida was no exception. Low pay attracted individuals of limited ability for the positions, with examples of the drunken or incompetent police officer being quite common. The quality of individuals recruited reflected the low esteem in which the police were held. The sheriffs were generally involved in both partisan politics and in enforcement of segregation. Minority police officers were rare until the 1950s.

Toward the end of the 19th century, the harmful impact of partisan politics was well recognized. The reform era emerged to address the involvement of politics in the administration of government. Many of the reforms, which were also directed at government, addressed problems with the police. Among these reforms were civil service protection for the police and insulation of the operation of the departments from extensive involvement from city councils and politics. During this era, the field of public administration was developing, and more progressive law enforcement practitioners were concerned about the poor reputation of their occupation. The response was to attempt to increase the qualifications of officers and to improve the status of the field in the eyes of the public.

To improve the police profession, in the first part of the 20th century the first baccalaureate program in criminology and police administration was established. Furthermore, the police increasingly advocated the use of scientific methods to solve crimes. The police also got out of the business of order maintenance because of the problems which the exercise of discretion caused them in the community. Increasingly, the police were asking that they be viewed as an emerging profession that aspired to the same status enjoyed by other professions. The police also improved their legitimacy by assuming responsibility for the level of crime in the community. During this era, the police developed tactics for directing resources toward the crime problem. As automobiles became less expensive and cities expanded, police cars were utilized to extend the amount of territory an officer could patrol. With the introduction of two-way radios, police officers' zones or areas of responsibility were further extended. The police also developed a doctrine based upon random patrols and rapid responses, which were thought to reduce the incidence of crime. Such an approach took the police out of day-to-day contact with citizens. The police now either patrolled or responded to calls and did not interact with the public on a regular basis.

POLICE MODELS

The Military Model

The departments in the early 20th century also implemented a military model of supervision. The rank structure was thought to provide the supervision required to control the freedom of the officers which historically had made them vulnerable to corruption and the misuse of power. Thus, initiative, which characterized the officer in the political era, was replaced by control in what is now characterized as the professional era. Unsupervised contact with the public was thought to be unprofessional and to open the door to opportunities for corruption.

The Professional Model

The professional model was focused on police visibility and apprehension. The rule of enforcement was emphasized, and police were clearly more reactive to crime. The law was followed without exception. Authoritative rules, a mechanistic organization structure, and strict guidelines controlled the police force. The impact of the professional model was significant. First, police increasingly were mobilized through the use of radios and patrol cars. Their response to the community became much more reactive. Second, the contact that the police had with "ordinary" citizens became much more limited. The police either associated with criminals or the victims of crime and had little contact with ordinary citizens. The response of the police was the development of cynical attitudes and an "us versus them" mentality and increasing amounts of stress. The impact of this on the mental health of police officers has been well documented in terms of increased incidence of alcohol and drug use, suicide, and marital problems.

Resetting Police Models

By the mid-1970s, crime rates had continued to rise and the resources devoted to the criminal justice system also had expanded. During this period, some forward-thinking police executives started questioning the effectiveness of some of the major principles of the professional model. In Kansas City, random patrol as a crime control strategy was questioned in a classical experimental design. Kansas was divided into three types of patrol areas. In one area, the police were withdrawn except to respond to calls for service; in another area, the police patrol levels were roughly tripled; and in the remaining area the patrol levels were kept the same. The citizens were extensively surveyed about their perceptions of safety and victimization before and after the experiment. After a 1-year period, the levels of crime and victimization were the same for each patrol area. These results cast serious questions about how police were utilized in the community (Police Foundation, 1974). Next, some police personnel questioned whether rapid response was effective in controlling crime. In four cities in different parts of the United States, it was determined that, unless an officer could be at the scene of a crime within 2 minutes of its commission, the clearance rate dropped to almost zero (Police Foundation, 1976). Another issue that received scrutiny was whether or not the resources devoted to investigations in fact resulted in crimes being solved. Examination of the effectiveness of police investigations revealed that relatively few crimes were being solved through investigations and that, for the most part, the information contained in the initial police report was recopied by the detectives.

The results of this research were a range of innovations in law enforcement. Some departments developed directed patrol strategies to put patrol officers into areas with high criminal activity to replace the use of random patrol. In regard to the response to calls for service, some departments developed differential response strategies. Rather than treating each call as being equally serious, these strategies categorized calls and directed police responses to them relative to the seriousness of the call. A life-threatening situation might result in a 1-minute response, while a barking dog might have to wait. Finally, in the area of investigations, police personnel identified *solvability* factors, which included items such as whether physical evidence or eyewitnesses were present and were used to determine whether or not an investigation would be pursued.

During this same period, the fear of crime was identified as a critical factor in the daily activities of citizens in the community. Perceptions of the crime rate in an area were used by citizens to modify their behavior. In some areas, they were becoming virtual prisoners in their homes, refusing to leave their residences at night or even sit on a porch. In many instances, it was determined that the fear of crime was greater than the actual probability of victimization. The result was that in Baltimore, Maryland, and Hartford, Connecticut, the police were directed to attempt to increase the perception of safety in a community by having more contacts with the citizenry and dealing with some of the public disorder in the streets (Moore and Trojanowicz, 1988).

In Flint, Michigan, the lack of contact with the police in the professional model of policing became a critical issue. In the late 1970s Flint, Michigan, received a grant from the Stewart Mott Foundation to place officers on walking beats in the city. The officers were assigned to specific geographical areas of responsibility rather than being shifted on a daily or weekly basis, as is the case with the professional patrol model. The model that emerged recognized that the majority of police officers' work is in the area of service. Officers work at developing knowledge and contacts with the citizens and promote the establishment of resources in the community to deal with community problems. The experiment, which was rigorously evaluated, established the validity of the program. While the crime rates did not decline significantly, calls for service were fewer and satisfaction with the police increased (Trojanowicz and Bucqueroux, 1990).

About the same time, in Madison, Wisconsin, Goldstein (1990) began analyzing the nature of police calls and determined that the calls were not randomly distributed throughout the city. It was determined that a small percentage of addresses were responsible for a majority of the calls for service. Furthermore, it was not uncommon for officers to go to an address 20 or 30 times for the same problem. In responding to the call, the officers would impose a disposition and then resume their patrol. Their actions represented a measure of productivity; they responded to a call and filed a report. Goldstein noted that much police work was reactive and that the actions of the officers did not solve the problem because the officers returned at some point in the future to the same address.

Goldstein determined that it might make sense for the police to reexamine their measures of productivity and to direct their resources at the recurring problems, which consumed much of their time. He proposed a series of analytical problem-solving steps that enabled the police to identify their recurring problems and to develop solutions. Fundamentally, the orientation was preventive rather than reactive. For example, in one area where cars were repeatedly being broken into, it was recognized that women were leaving their purses in their cars to go to a dance club. The officer who was assigned to the problem suggested to the club owner that lockers be installed. This provided security for the women's purses and reduced the opportunities for thefts to occur.

FLORIDA AND THE ERAS OF POLICING

Florida was thinly populated along the coast until the early part of this century. The climate and disease made large portions of the state uninhabitable. By the 1920s, the completion of railroads to Tampa and Miami made the southwest and eastern portions of the state more accessible to vacationers from the north and land speculators. However, only after World War II and the invention of the air conditioner did a large number of people move into Florida. In many of the larger cities in Florida, the professional era of policing existed only for perhaps 20 years before the conditions were created for them to experiment with the community policing model (see next section).

By the start of the 1980s, Florida had caught up with the rest of the United States and in some respects exceeded the rest of the country in the implementation of community police models. The legacy of segregation resulted in many areas having separate black communities, which were historically neglected in terms of receiving an equitable share of governmental resources. As recently as the early 1960s, blacks were prohibited from being in certain parts of many cities after dark. Although such behavior was legally prohibited, anecdotal evidence exists of officers arresting and otherwise harassing members of the black community into the early 1970s.

Riots were a recurring problem in Miami in the early and mid-1980s. These were precipitated by questions relating to the use of deadly force and the perception of racial discrimination in the administration of justice. Furthermore, in many of the larger urban areas, historically black areas were suffering an exodus of the professionals who were once bound to the areas through segregation. With the stabilizing influences leaving and immigrants from the Caribbean and Central America causing further changes in these communities, the result was the creation of inner-city areas that faced significant problems and limited resources.

EVOLUTION OF THE COMMUNITY POLICING MODEL

By the mid-1980s, many departments were beginning to question the premises on which the professional model of policing was based and began to develop what has come to be termed "community policing." During this same period, the conceptual framework within which the community policing model was embedded began to expand. It was recognized that the structure of the community in which the community policing program was organized was an important determinant of the need for police services (Skogan, 1990).

In many communities that are stable and have relatively small crime problems, residents share standards about appropriate behavior and regulate their behavior accordingly. In communities with significant crime and delinquency problems, the formal and informal social control mechanisms that make communities orderly, respectable, and predictable places to live have broken down (Skogan, 1990). This decline in social control creates conditions where property is abandoned, drugs are openly bought and sold, prostitutes congregate, and trash is discarded. The impact of this disorder is significant on the residents of a community. Those who can leave do so, while those who cannot, retreat from the streets, leaving them to undesirable elements. This in turn sets the stage for the crime rate in an area to increase as problem populations, with little concern for community standards, encroach into an area. A cycle of decline in an area sets in that impacts the decisions of businesses to invest, homeowners to buy and sell, and families with children to locate into other areas with schools that command quality educational resources.

The shift to community policing typically requires the vision of a new relationship between the police and the community. The police no longer accept sole responsibility for the crime problem. Correspondingly, the police recognize that they must shift their behavior to create a partnership with the community. This requires the creation of a strategic plan and a strategy to change the organization. At least in theory, this should come before the implementation of the program.

Significant differences between the community policing model and the professional model can be identified; some of these differences are outlined in the table provided here.

COMMUNITY POLICING AND TRADITIONAL POLICING

Community Policing Model	Professional Model
Focus on community	Focus on police
Problem oriented	Incident driven
Proactive	Reactive
Uses all information: *Uniform Crime Report,* census, neighborhood groups	Uses crime-related information
Invokes public/private organizations as primary intervention; criminal justice system, last	Invokes criminal justice system
Uses statistics and community data	Uses criminal justice system data
Analysis and innovation from the bottom up	Top down organization
Deals with problems not symptoms	Deals with symptoms not problems

COMMUNITY POLICING IN FLORIDA

In the past 5 years, most major police jurisdictions in Florida have experimented with implementing community policing programs. Programs can be identified in Orlando, Tallahassee, St. Petersburg, West Palm Beach, Miami, and the Broward Sheriff's Office. The evolution of these developments has been very decentralized. Typically, there is some public demand for community policing, although what actually constitutes community policing is not well defined. The programs that have been implemented range from simply putting some new decals on one or two cars to starting "walk and talk" programs. In others, the officers may be sent to 1 or 2 days of school and then told to implement a community policing program in the department.

In Palm Beach County, almost every department has at least one officer engaged in community policing. A community police officers' organization has been created to promote community policing and to provide support and new ideas to officers.

Sometimes the work of community police officers is not characterized as real police work. In Broward County, the sheriff's office is implementing community policing at the departmental level, representing perhaps the most ambitious application of this philosophy in Florida.

Despite these advances, there has been little encouragement from the state regarding promulgation of community policing. The Florida Department of Law Enforcement has implemented 40-hour blocks of training for crime prevention officers; however, no comparable level of support or certification exists at the state level for community policing.

Community policing requires a significant reorientation in how departments conduct their activities. In other parts of the country, including Portland, Oregon, and Madison, Wisconsin, this change was preceded by a process of strategic planning. For the most part, community policing is being implemented in departments that carry out activities consistent with both the professional model and the emerging model of strategic planning and change. It is difficult, if not impossible, to determine the extent of the commitment to community policing or the amount of organizational change that is desired. Results of implementing community policing are for the most part very mixed in the departments attempting it.

The picture that emerges is that the current strategies used by law enforcement in Florida are not likely to lead to a significant reduction in the levels of crime in communities or improve the relationship between police departments and the community. The evolution of community policing is based on questioning of many of the tenets of the professional model and replacing them with those in the community policing model. The elements of this model are not completely defined but include the following components:

1. In the professional model, the police have assumed responsibility for controlling the crime problem in the community. This goal is recognized as impossible to achieve in the community policing model. In the community policing model, crime is viewed as a complex social problem that requires the creation of a partnership between the police and the community to resolve the problem of crime and delinquency.

2. The professional model, with its emphasis on reactive enforcement strategies, has taken the police out of contact with the community. The community police response takes the uncommitted time of the police and the time spent in random police patrol and redirects it toward establishing a relationship between the police and the citizens of the community. The police in partnership with the community assume responsibility for a social area such as a neighborhood.

3. Community policing represents a philosophy and is not another special program such as police community relations or crime prevention. It represents a fundamental shift in the orientation of the department and recognizes the importance of establishing relationships with community institutions that strengthen the ability of communities to function effectively. This includes community education strategies, community development, neighborhood organization, economic development, and so forth.

One of the premises upon which community policing is based is recognition that communities and neighborhoods are social organizations whose health must be addressed. Typically, government looks at the physical structures and spatial layouts of communities and then develops comprehensive plans. Community policing alters that view and argues that policing must be viewed in relation to other social institutions in the community. As a result, crime and delinquency are viewed in relation to the social infrastructure of the community. This means that a community's schools, housing stock, level of economic development, demographic and social characteristics, physical structure, and level of political organization should be assessed in relation to the crime problems in the community.

Political and organizational structures of government are also relatively fragmented and isolated. Frequently, governmental agencies do not have the ability to coordinate their responses to problems (Wiatrowski, 1995). Government should develop more of a team approach to the issue of community development. It is unlikely that the traditional bureaucratized approaches to municipal government can cut across the compartmentalization that exists. To counteract this, government leaders should explore new methods of cooperating to confront problems in the community. Work in the area of reinventing government has significant implications for this aspect of community policing.

Florida, as one of the most rapidly growing states, has many of the conditions that make it reasonable to consider community policing. First, the rapid growth of the state means that many communities are in a state of transition. Older neighborhoods may require stabilization, while newer communities frequently lack any kind of social organization. Second, the large minority involvement in crime is frequently viewed without examining the sources of the problem. The disproportionate involvement of minorities in crime is generally not examined in relation to the environment in which the children grow up. In Lake Worth, two significant developments have taken place. In one venture, community police officers have involved high-risk minority youths in working with law enforcement officers as clerks; of the 16 youths who participated in the program over a 2-year period, none was arrested. Also, several community police officers have been trained as code enforcement officers who have the ability to investigate landlords who are maintaining substandard residences and in many cases violating zoning laws. For example, some landlords have been known to sublet a house with three bedrooms to three separate families. The impact on the neighborhood and adjacent property values can be substantial. Those who take pride in their homes would see the value of their investments deteriorate because of the code violations and the attendant increases in traffic, garbage, parked cars, etc.

The relationship between the drug problem and declining communities has been reviewed by Johnson et al. (1990). The link between drugs and crime has been well established in decaying, historically minority areas. There are few indications that current enforcement approaches are effective in controlling these problems, and a community based approach may be more effective. In West Palm Beach, for example, the familiarity between the police force and small-scale drug users has led police to develop employment alternatives for "dime-bag sellers."

In some parts of Florida, the "full-service school" concept is being used as a basis for community policing. This is a significant development because it stresses the central role of schools in assessing and responding to community problems. Community police officers in Delray Beach have involved unsupervised children in the community in after-school programs. They also tell parents about the public health and adult literacy programs at the school in an effort to improve the quality and accessibility of health care in the community.

CONCLUSION

The development of law enforcement in the United States is an outgrowth of two divergent trends. First, geographical distances that separated population areas have resulted in a strong tradition of local autonomy in law enforcement. Second, by the 1840s, the impact of urbanization had rendered traditional methods of social control such as sheriffs and night watchmen ineffective. In the 1980s, many departments began to question the premises on which the professional model of policing was based and initiated development of what has come to be termed "community policing." Significant differences can be identified between community policing and the traditional professional model.

DISCUSSION QUESTIONS

1. How can the police and communities work together more effectively?

2. How can new forms of intergovernmental cooperation be fostered?

3. How can neighborhood and community organizations be organized more effectively?

4. How can communities and governments be encouraged to develop preventive rather than reactive strategies to combat crime and delinquency problems in the community?

5. What recommendations can be made to enhance trust between members of the community and police officers?

REFERENCES

Federal Bureau of Investigation (FBI). 1990. *Crime in the United States: Uniform Crime Report.* Washington, D.C.: Federal Bureau of Investigation, U.S. Government Printing Office.

Goldstein, H. 1990. *Problem Oriented Policing.* New York: McGraw-Hill.

Johnson, B. D., T. Williams, K. A. Dei, and H. Sanabria. 1990. Drug abuse in the inner city: impact on hard-drug users and the community, in M. Tonry and J. Q. Wilson, eds., *Crime and Justice: A Review of Research.* Chicago: University of Chicago Press.

Moore, M. and R. Trojanowicz. 1988. *Policing and the Fear of Crime.* Washington, D.C.: National Institute of Justice and Harvard University.

Police Foundation. 1974. *Report on Crime Control.* Washington, D.C.: The Police Foundation.

Police Foundation. 1976. *Report on Crime Control.* Washington, D.C.: The Police Foundation.

Rand Corporation. 1994. *The Impact of Three Strikes and You're Out.* Santa Monica, Calif.: unpublished report.

Skogan, W. 1990. *Disorder and Decline.* New York: Free Press.

Trojanowicz, R. and B. Bucqueroux. 1990. *Community Policing.* Cincinnati, Ohio: Anderson.

Wiatrowski, M. D. 1995. An evaluation of the Delray Beach community police program, in *Community Policing,* P. Kratcoski, ed., Cincinnati, Ohio: Anderson.

Community Crime Prevention Model

PURPOSE

The Community Crime Prevention Model (CCPM) will serve as a catalyst to provide the community and all its stakeholders with a comprehensive and inclusive process designed to improve the communication level of all stakeholders and develop strategies concerning the prevention and reduction of crime, the fear of crime, violence, drug abuse, and disorder. Focusing on these quality of life issues will lead to greater involvement on the part of all stakeholders to positively impact society.

GOALS

The focal goals of the CCPM are as follows:

- The model will serve to improve the overall feeling of security among all stakeholders, therefore improving quality of life concerns within respective communities.

- The model will provide the appropriate structure in which the community, partnering with other stakeholders and governmental agencies, will be active participants in the design, implementation, and assessment of problem-solving strategies intended to improve quality-of-life issues and concerns.

- The model will provide the suitable structure that will facilitate and foster open lines of communication among all participants (all stakeholders), therefore simultaneously working to improve the level of trust and credibility within the respective groups.

- The model's structure will both formally and informally provide an environment of accountability in order to effectively guide the participants to remain within the scope and purpose of the model's design.

RATIONALE OF MODEL

History teaches us that the relationship between the police and the community has been a difficult one. In recent years, there has been a constant struggle to improve communication between the two groups. The police (paramilitary organization) and police subculture create an environment of closed-mindedness and distrust. Any group that does not come from within the organization is not trusted. As this attitude permeates throughout the organization, police personnel perceive a wrongful belief system of thinking that any non-police personnel cannot possibly understand their concerns. This unhealthy belief system is further institutionalized when political officials attack the police by pandering to special-interest groups. In the end, the silent majority (overall community) suffers from the backlash of police misconduct and overall distrust.

A variety of very good programs (Team Police, Weed and Seed, Community Policing, etc.) have attempted to bridge this chasm of miscommunication between the police and the community. These programs, although at times effective, do not reach the breadth and depth of the problem. An unhealthy attitude and level of mistrust between the groups, if not properly addressed, over time will adversely impact any new program created. An example can be illustrated by the Community-Oriented Policing and Problem Solving (COPPS) program. Department after department became participants of the COPPS program solely to use the funds attached to the program. Across the nation, police departments created special units funded by the COPS grant and placed them to work with a larger work force not trained in the community-oriented policing philosophy. A conflict between policing models arose, creating strained relationships among the two groups, in addition to damaging the police community relationships among the larger group not trained in community policing strategies. The relationship further deteriorated when administrations were still requiring statistics (arrests, traffic citations, etc.) to evaluate the officers' performance. One group was being evaluated according to community-oriented policing philosophies while the larger police force was being evaluated using traditional methodologies.

These programs failed to address the root of the problem and, furthermore, did not have the proper strategies in place to change unhealthy attitudes within an entrenched subculture. In addition, they failed to address the issue from a top-down perspective. Unhealthy attitudes toward community relations must first be addressed within leadership positions. Military history illustrates that individuals will generally follow a leader's direction and vision.

Overall, these community programs were not successful because they failed to address the following issues:

- They failed to establish a sense of urgency and need for immediate attention.

- They lacked the vision and design of proper strategies needed to address major obstacles such as entrenched subcultures.

- They failed to create a strong coalition of support, very much needed to remove major obstacles such as executives not possessing the desired vision.

- They failed to communicate their vision by not properly educating, training, and disseminating the desired vision to leadership positions first, before attempting to train employees.

- They failed to empower employees who shared the desired vision, thus stunting the growth and progress of the vision.

- They failed to reward and celebrate short-term wins while remaining focused on the desired long-term vision.

- They failed to create changes within the systems, structures, and infrastructure of the organization (they did not produce long-lasting changes inside the organization).

- They failed to establish any changes in the culture of the organization (the unhealthy side of the culture remained regardless of the programs being generated).

- They failed to establish a structured model that focuses on changing the infrastructure and culture of organizations by a process of constant communication, accountability, and adaptability to a changing environment.

To complicate matters, survey data, including the recently released *Are We Safe? 2000* survey conducted by Wirthlin Worldwide on behalf of the National Crime Prevention Council and ADT Security, have demonstrated that, despite the fact that crime is down, there are still significant numbers of individuals who fear being victimized by crime (particularly women and minorities); individuals are less engaged in their communities (volunteering less and less aware of crime prevention programs); and most parents remain concerned about the safety of their children at school and in the community but do not always follow through to ensure their safety and, in fact, are supervising their children far less than in the past. We still have significant work to do in order to prevent being victimized by crime and to ensure a safe and secure future for our children. The solutions will be found in our families, schools, and communities. Creating lasting changes in these domains should be the primary objective of community crime prevention. Although crime rates are currently low, there is reason for concern. Researchers suggest that over the next several years we may see crime begin to increase in many of our cities. Further, many of our nation's hardest-hit communities have not enjoyed the dramatic decreases witnessed by other communities. Many communities have simply been left behind (National Comprehensive Crime Prevention Act, 1999).

Our nation's population doubled from 1947 to 2000. This reality, coupled with growing disparity between the richest and poorest populations, is causing the spread of urban crime problems traditionally associated with the more densely populated northern states to other regions of the country. Such growth has contributed to the loosening of community bonds and created more isolation—both powerful contributors to crime. Crime, violence, and drug abuse prevention must become a reality for urban, rural, and frontier environments. This is both a big city issue and a small city issue. Crime, violence, and drug abuse are becoming geographically and demographically seamless (National Comprehensive Crime Prevention Act, 1999).

The combination of poor community police relations coupled with constant changes in the environment, police racial profiling, persistent fear of crime within communities, illicit drug use, and the poor not progressing economically at the same level as other classes are tearing at the very foundation and fiber of society. Communities across the nation need the proper assistance in order to develop synergistic and effective crime prevention strategies. The Community Crime Prevention Model will provide the proper framework and necessary structure to help address these maladies. The model will assist communities nationwide to develop crime prevention strategies while focusing simultaneously on improving police community relations. This focus will in turn foster community involvement, open lines of communication between the police and community, and create an overall improvement in quality-of-life concerns.

DESCRIPTION OF MODEL

As previously described, the Community Crime Prevention Model (CCPM) will serve as a catalyst to provide the community, and its various stakeholders, with a comprehensive and inclusive process designed to improve communication and develop innovative and responsive strategies concerning the prevention and reduction of crime. The model will facilitate the design and implementation of crime prevention methodologies while working to foster open lines of communication between the police and the community.

The CCPM has various strengths and attributes that address current shortcomings in crime prevention. Some of these shortcomings include a lack of communication among all participants, inadequate coordination and responsiveness, lack of vision, and inadequate accountability measures. In contrast, the major strength of the CCPM is that it places stakeholders as active participants in the crime prevention process. In fact, with the CCPM, stakeholders become key participants in the design, implementation, and assessment of crime prevention strategies with a focus on improving quality of life concerns (please refer to Table of Organization).

The following is a step-by-step process of the CCPM:

1. Community stakeholders informally, or formally, identify a concern or idea for further review and consideration. Stakeholders with issues or concerns may take their idea or issue directly to the appropriate agency or they may forward the concern or idea to the Crime Prevention Advisory Council (please refer to Table of Organization). The Crime Prevention Advisory Council will meet with the community bimonthly at a district level to hear ideas and concerns and to provide progress updates on the status of ongoing projects being worked on.

2. This concern or idea is then forwarded to the Crime Prevention Advisory Council (one of three components of the Community Crime Prevention Coalition), which will hear the community ideas and concerns and process the information.

3. The idea or concern is then forwarded to the Crime Prevention Clearinghouse for classification and inclusion in the database. All ideas and concerns will be recorded to provide a base for further research and to develop appropriate strategies.

4. The concern or idea, if warranted (the problem may have previously been addressed), is then forwarded to the Crime Prevention Problem Assessment Committee for further review and action. The Crime Prevention Problem Assessment Committee will then evaluate forwarded ideas and assess the nature and severity of any listed problem. The committee will then make referrals to the proper agencies for problem resolution or idea implementation.

5. Once an idea or problem has been properly addressed by the Community Crime Prevention Coalition (please refer to Table of Organization) this information will be forwarded to the State Crime Prevention Council, which acts as a liaison, advisory, and oversight body for all community crime prevention programs and strategies using the Community Crime Prevention Model. The agency handling the problem or further evaluating the idea will report the appropriate strategy, as well as the corresponding progress made to the Crime Prevention Clearinghouse. This process will ensure that all ideas and problems processed by the Community Crime Prevention Model are fairly implemented and evaluated according to the philosophy of the model. The Crime Prevention Clearinghouse will report periodically to the Crime Prevention Advisory Council the status of the various ongoing projects to ensure program integrity and continuity, as well as ensure that stakeholder needs are being met. The Crime Prevention Advisory Council will provide the community a status report on a bimonthly basis of the ongoing projects currently being worked on. This will serve to keep the community

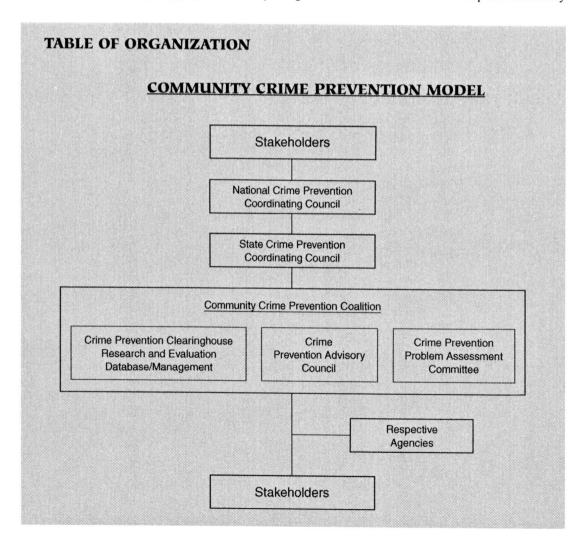

TABLE OF ORGANIZATION

COMMUNITY CRIME PREVENTION MODEL

well informed and constantly aware of the progress of all ideas, concerns, and projected resolutions.

6. Each State Crime Prevention Council will periodically provide a summary of ongoing projects to the National Crime Prevention Coordinating Council for the purpose of keeping a national record of community concerns and crime prevention ideas. This methodology will provide a steady flow of data to track, map out, and conduct further research on issues dealing with community concerns and crime prevention. In addition, the National Crime Prevention Coordinating Council, when needed, will have the data available to report community trends from micro and macro perspectives.

The Community Crime Prevention Model (CCPM) will encourage strategic data-driven planning and the development and implementation of research-based policies and programs that promote and encourage communities to develop comprehensive and inclusive crime prevention initiatives. These efforts will encourage the establishment of performance standards and goals for crime prevention and crime reduction. The program elements of this act are anchored in the fundamental belief that crime prevention is everybody's business.

The model will promote the necessary structure and foundation to engage grassroots communities in problem identification and problem-solving strategies. The design of the model also will act to promote and motivate policymakers at national, state, and local levels of government to provide the necessary leadership required to create functional and environmental changes that will promote community well-being and improve quality-of-life issues.

OVERVIEW OF PROCESS

The Community Crime Prevention Model needs to be supported by government at the national, state, and local levels. Without this support, the infrastructure of the model promoting accountability will be debilitated. Police departments and other governmental agencies will be less likely to support and be fully involved in all aspects of the model without political support from national, state, and local levels. This document will help to express the need and sense of urgency within our communities on issues such as crime prevention, quality-of-life issues, and police community relations.

The Community Crime Prevention Model, if properly enacted, develops both a purposeful vision and inclusive strategies for the purpose of improving community police relations, crime prevention methodologies, and quality-of-life concerns. This model will also help to change the role the community plays within our system by providing a structured methodology that encourages continuous communication among the community, police, and government officials.

The following sequence of events will help support the success of the Community Crime Prevention Model:

1. Acquire political support at the national and state levels. This will later be extremely beneficial in acquiring the necessary support at the local political level.

2. Acquire the funds necessary to enact the model (it is possible to start with a pilot project in order to measure success and create momentum).

3. Conduct a series of Train the Trainer sessions for the training staff of the National Crime Prevention Council. The sessions will include a full explanation of the Community Crime Prevention Model and also incorporate John P. Kotter's "Eight-Stage Process of Creating Change" to provide the proper climate of change and inspiration.

4. The staff from the National Crime Prevention Council will then pilot this model at the most suitable location. If it is successful, the National Crime Prevention Council will implement training in this model nationwide.

THE COMMUNITY CRIME PREVENTION MODEL DEFINITIONS

1. *Stakeholders:* For the purpose of this model, stakeholders shall include all community members, including citizens, private sector groups or organizations, non-governmental organizations, various governmental entities, and civic groups.

2. *National Crime Prevention Coordinating Council:* The National Crime Prevention Coordinating Council will be an advisory and oversight body, designed to act as a liaison in support of crime prevention strategies at the state level. It will act as a forum for the exchange of ideas and information concerning community crime prevention and various related policing issues at the national level.

3. *State Crime Prevention Coordinating Council:* The State Crime Prevention Coordinating Council will be an advisory, oversight, and coordinating body, designed to act as a liaison in support of crime prevention strategies at the local level. It will act as a forum for the exchange of ideas and information concerning community crime prevention and various related policing issues at the state level.

4. *Community Crime Prevention Coalition:* The Community Crime Prevention Coalition will encompass the Crime Prevention Advisory Council, Crime Prevention Clearinghouse, and Crime Prevention Assessment Committee and will act to coordinate, monitor, assess, research, and record crime prevention strategies and related policing issues at the local level.

5. *Crime Prevention Advisory Council:* The Crime Prevention Council will be represented by a wide array of community representatives from all walks of life. The council will also have local governmental representation to include county commissioners, police executives, code enforcement, etc.

6. *Crime Prevention Problem Assessment Committee:* The Crime Prevention Problem Assessment Committee will be represented by a wide array of community representatives with experience in assessing community problems and policing concerns. The committee will assess ideas and concerns from stakeholders and make the appropriate referral to respective agencies.

7. *Crime Prevention Clearinghouse:* The Crime Prevention Clearinghouse will act as a research body designed to record all ideas and concerns raised by the community. The database will monitor the progress of all ideas and concerns to ensure accountability.

CHAPTER 3

Crime and Victims in Florida

CHAPTER OVERVIEW

This chapter provides the student with an overview of the methods by which crimes are counted. The State of Florida, through the Florida Department of Law Enforcement, has a centralized clearinghouse that collects crime data from law enforcement agencies. Crimes in the State of Florida are defined and classified in this chapter, and the formula for calculating crime rates is provided and discussed. Issues and objectives pertaining to the Florida Uniform Crime Reports Programs are reviewed.

CRIMES

A *crime* is the commission of an act in violation of a law. Laws also provide and authorize punishment for such actions. It must be noted that laws vary greatly with time, jurisdictional locations, and circumstances; however, this chapter maintains its focus on Florida.

Crimes in Florida can be placed in two general categories: A *felony* is a serious crime or offense that is punishable by one or more years in prison, and a misdemeanor is a less serious crime that is punishable by less than one year in the county jail. The *Florida Law Enforcement Handbook* (1999) defines the term *felony* as any criminal offense that is punishable under the laws of this state, or that would be punishable if committed in this state, by death or imprisonment in a state penitentiary. State penitentiary shall include state correctional facilities. A person shall be imprisoned in the state penitentiary for each sentence, which except for an extended term, exceeds one year. The term *misdemeanor* shall mean any criminal offense that is punishable under the laws of this state, or that would be punishable if committed in this state, by a term of imprisonment in a county correctional facility, except for an extended term, not in excess of one year. The term crime shall mean a felony or misdemeanor.

CLASSIFYING FELONIES

Felonies within the State of Florida are classified for the purpose of sentencing in five categories (*Florida Law Enforcement Handbook*, 1999):

1. Capital felony

2. Life felony

3. Felony of the first degree

4. Felony of the second degree

5. Felony of the third degree

CLASSIFYING MISDEMEANORS

Misdemeanors are also classified for the purpose of sentencing in two categories:

1. Misdemeanor of the first degree

2. Misdemeanor of the second degree

(*Source: Florida Law Enforcement Handbook,* 1999.)

COUNTING CRIME

Nationally, crime is counted by way of two major sources: the *Uniform Crime Report* (UCR) and the *National Crime Survey* (NCS). The UCR is published by the Federal Bureau of Investigation and obtains its data from police agencies. Each month, the law enforcement agencies report the frequency of crime—that is, the number of Part I offenses (see the eight offenses listed in the table) that have occurred within their jurisdiction. The NCS is conducted by the Bureau of Justice Statistics and is based not on police reports but on interviews with persons in about 60,000 households each 6 months.

THE UNIFORM CRIME REPORT (PART I OFFENSES)

Crimes reported	Homicide
	Rape
	Robbery
	Assault
	Burglary
	Larceny
	Motor vehicle theft
	Arson
Scope of crime	Crimes reported to the police
Collection	Police report crime count to a centralized state agency that reports to the FBI
Sponsor	Department of Justice
	Federal Bureau of Investigation

(*Source:* FBI, 1998.)

NATIONAL CRIME SURVEY

Crime measured	Rape
	Robbery
	Assault
	Household burglary
	Larceny
	Motor vehicle theft
Scope of crime	Crimes reported to the police and crimes not reported to the police
Collection	Survey interviews; persons 12 years of age and older
Sponsor	Department of Justice
	Bureau of Justice Statistics

(*Source:* Bureau of Justice Statistics, 1998.)

METHODS OF COUNTING CRIME

The Crime Index

It is important to understand that the UCR is divided into two parts: Part I crimes and Part II crimes. Part I offenses consist of the index crimes that are considered more serious in nature. This index includes murder, forcible rape, robbery, aggravated assault, burglary, larceny, motor vehicle theft, and arson. Part II crimes are considered less serious and are often discounted when calculating crime rates. The non-indexed offenses consist of a variety of crimes (the UCR addresses 22 crimes). This group may include crimes of simple assault, minor damage from vandalism, disorderly conduct, and trespassing.

The Crime Rate

The crime rate for Florida is calculated using the crime index for Part I crimes. The purpose of the index is to provide a composite dimension, by allowing a view of the eight categories of offenses. This general approach provides an overview of crime in selected jurisdictions, however, crime rates for other types of crime (such as the murder crime rate for Miami) can be obtained by using the following calculation:

$$\frac{\text{Number of crimes}}{\text{Population}} \times 100,000 = \text{Crime rate}$$

Example: The county of Palm Beach experienced 80,143 Part I crimes in one calendar year, and the population was recorded as 918,223:

$$\frac{80,143}{918,223} \times 100,000 = 8728$$

Palm Beach County has a crime rate of 8728 per 100,000 residents.

Example: The county of Miami–Dade experienced 368 murders in one calendar year, and the population was reported as 2,037,566:

$$\frac{368}{2,037,566} \times 100,000 = 18$$

Miami–Dade County has a murder rate of 18 per 100,000 residents.

This calculation allows for control of the number of people, and it provides a fair comparison of different-sized jurisdictions to one another. A jurisdiction with a crime rate of 5556 compared to a jurisdiction with a crime rate of 8445 indicates that the latter location has more crime or criminal activity. The rate is expressed as crimes occurring within the selected jurisdiction per 100,000 people.

THE FLORIDA DEPARTMENT OF LAW ENFORCEMENT

The State of Florida established the *Uniform Crime Report* statute in 1967. This law mandated that the Florida Department of Law Enforcement (FDLE) would be responsible for the collection of crime data and authorized to disseminate this information. In 1971, the FDLE began the systematic collection of crime data from police agencies throughout the state.

In 1986, Florida amended Chapter 943, mandating the expansion of the scope of collectable crime data. This change now requires police to report information on the type of crime, offenders' information, arrests, and victims. The new and expanded information provides insight into classifications of people who commit crime in the state; arrests by age, sex, and race; and domestic violence reports, along with other descriptive data. The document prepared by the FDLE, entitled *Crime in Florida,* is designed to disseminate accurate crime information.

The Florida Uniform Crime Report program is designed to:

- inform the governor, cabinet, legislature, criminal justice and other governmental officials, and the general public as to the nature of the crime problem in Florida, its magnitude, and its trends

- provide policymakers with a sound statistical basis for planning and guiding the criminal justice community

- provide law enforcement administrators with crime statistics for administrative and operational use

- describe the attributes of crimes and victims in order to help determine the proper focus for prevention and to assist in measuring the effectiveness of prevention programs

- describe the characteristics of arrested offenders and their offenses in order to develop the proper focus for enforcement efforts and to assist in measuring the effectiveness of targeted enforcement and deterrence programs

- provide base data and statistics for research to understand crime in this state and to assist criminal justice agencies in the performance of their duties

- provide base data for the determination of law enforcement manpower and training needs

- provide data to assist in the assessment of the causes of crime for the development of theories of criminal behavior

- provide other states and federal criminal justice agencies with Florida crime data

(*Source:* FDLE, 2000.)

Although the Federal Bureau of Investigation assumes responsibility for the publication of the *Uniform Crime Report,* the Florida Department of Law Enforcement compiles and acts as a clearinghouse for crimes within the state. All law enforcement agencies throughout the state report the seven index offenses of murder, rape, robbery, aggravated assault, burglary, larceny, and motor vehicle theft. Florida also has an additional eight mandatory reportable crimes: manslaughter, kidnap/abduction, arson, simple assault, drug/narcotic offenses, bribery, embezzlement, and fraud. The FDLE provides local police agencies an option to report counterfeiting/forgery, extortion/blackmail, intimidation, nonforcible sex offenses, stolen property (buying, receiving, possessing), driving under the influence, destruction/damage/vandalism of property, gambling offenses, weapons violations, and liquor law violations.

FLORIDA INDEX OFFENSES

Homicide/murder	Causing the death of another person without legal justification
Forcible sex offenses	Unlawful forced sexual intercourse, rape, sodomy, and fondling
Robbery	The unlawful taking or attempted taking of property by force or threat of force that is in the immediate possession of another
Aggravated assault	Unlawful intentional inflicting of serious bodily injury or the unlawful threat or attempt to inflict bodily injury or death by means of a deadly dangerous weapon
Burglary	Unlawful entry of a structure or a conveyance with the intent to commit an offense
Larceny	Knowingly obtain or use or endeavor to obtain or to use, temporarily or permanently, the property of another
Motor vehicle theft	Unlawful taking or attempted taking of a self-propelled vehicle owned by another

(*Source:* FDLE, 2000.)

Florida Police Agencies

With the advent of contracting police services from sheriffs' offices and in some areas the incorporation of new jurisdictions, the total number of law enforcement agencies fluctuates. Approximately 386 police agencies submit crime data to the FDLE. The State of Florida has 66 county law enforcement agencies, approximately 295 local police agencies, 10 university police departments, 5 state law enforcement agencies, 3 county school police departments, 4 airport police agencies, and the Seminole and Miccosukee Indian police (FDLE, 2000). The report (FDLE, 2000) has provided guidelines for the various law enforcement agencies, such as crime and arrests should not be counted by more than one agency; local police count crime and arrests within city limits; sheriffs' offices count crime and arrests within unincorporated county areas or areas not included within a city; and state agencies count crime and arrests affected by their personnel. It is important to note that the *Uniform Crime Report* utilizes a hierarchical scale for many multiple offense reports. It reports one offense per victim; however, if a report contains multiple crimes for one victim, the UCR will select the highest crime for the crime count (see Chapter 2 for an explanation of the police system in Florida).

REPORTING CRIME TO THE POLICE

The *National Crime Survey* indicates that only about 37% of all personal and household crimes are reported to the police. Reported crime impacts the workload of the police, the chance of arrest, and the *Uniform Crime Report*. When citizens fail to report a crime to law enforcement, the police cannot investigate nor do they have the opportunity to solve or prosecute the offender. Some of the reasons for not reporting personal and household victimization to police are provided in the table.

REASONS FOR NOT REPORTING CRIMES

Reason	All Personal Crimes (%)	Crimes of Violence (%)	All Household Crimes (%)
Attempt/no loss	25.8	20.4	32.3
Private matter	7.3	4.8	4.1
Reported to another official	15.5	21.7	5.3
Not important	2.8	9.4	3.9
Not aware of crime	4.3	0.3	7.1
No way to identify property	6.9	0.3	7.7
Lack of proof	10.7	6.5	11.4
Police would not want to be bothered	6.5	6.8	9.0
Insurance will cover it	21.0	0.1	1.9
Police would be inefficient/ineffective	2.7	4.6	4.0

(*Source: National Crime Survey Report,* 1990.)

THE POPULATION OF FLORIDA

The population of Florida is reported by the Division of Population Studies, Bureau of Economic and Business Research, at the University of Florida. The crime rate figures use a resident population figure of about 15,982,378, which is far less than the estimated 31,000,000 additional visitors each year. The official crime rate can be affected by many factors, one of which is the number of visitors to Florida. The number of people during the winter season may distort the crime rate. The number of potential victims and offenders increases with the volume of visitors. Tourism is the main industry of the state. Florida publishes information monthly and annually about visitors; it is estimated that, on any given day, about 1.34 million tourists are visiting the state, with an average length of 13.6 days. In terms of offender mobility, the FDLE reports indicate that approximately 10% of all arrests in Broward County were nonresidents. This issue, among many others, is an example of how neither the UCR nor the NCS provides an absolutely accurate crime picture.

CRIME IN FLORIDA

In reviewing the 79 urban areas across the country with more than 500,000 residents, Miami–Dade County has ranked at or near the top over the last 10 years. Residents are victimized at a rate of about 12 serious crimes for every 100 people. Nationally, in the late 1990s, Miami–Dade County ranked first in aggravated assault, burglary, and larceny. The county ranked second in robbery and auto theft and eleventh in murder. Florida's southern counties experienced a crime rate more than double the national average.

The southern section of the state, including Miami–Dade, Broward, and Palm Beach counties, contains a diverse population of over 4.2 million permanent residents. All three counties continue to lead the nation in crime. Prosecutors, police, corrections personnel, and academicians offer the following explanations for the high crime rates:

- *Drugs:* The drug business (users, sellers, financiers, smugglers, and transporters) contributes substantially to the violent crime rate.

- *Guns:* Guns are easy to get in South Florida. Many are associated with the drug business. Juveniles find easy handgun access useful for settling disputes.

- *Prisons:* Florida's prisons and jails are overcrowded. Courts continue to mandate premature release for violent offenders.

- *The elderly:* South Florida has a population permeated with retired people. Some communities are entirely made up of the elderly. These communities may provide the criminal with the perception of easy targets.

- *Weather:* The southern metro areas have always reported a higher crime rate than the north. Many attribute increased crime to the warm climate, as outdoor activity provides more opportunity for disputes and confrontation.

- *Diversity of class:* Very affluent population contrasts with poverty in South Florida. Low-compensating service-oriented jobs are compounded by unemployment problems.

- *Ethnic diversity:* Racial and ethnic tensions emerge from an urban setting that consists of many different backgrounds.

VIOLENT CRIME RANKINGS

Murder, Rape, Robbery, and Aggravated Assault Combined

Rank	Location	Population	Crime Rate per 100,000
1	New York City	7,375,097	2163.7
2	Miami–Dade, Fla.	2,019,426	2037.0
3	Los Angeles, Calif.	9,193,319	1778.6
4	Miami–Dade, Broward, and Palm Beach, Fla.	4,228,464	1524.7
5	Jacksonville, Fla.	945,413	1440.5
6	Little Rock, Ark.	523,823	1372.8
7	Baltimore, Md.	2,445,286	1359.4
8	New Orleans, La.	1,258,657	1326.7
9	Tampa, Fla.	2,156,055	1268.3
10	Springfield, Mass.	540,224	1231.2
13	Palm Beach, Fla.	900,197	1169.0
30	Broward, Fla.	1,308,841	978.9

Murder

Rank	Location	Murder Rate per 100,000
1	New Orleans, La.	28.3
2	New York City	27.1
3	Los Angeles, Calif.	20.9
4	Birmingham, Ala.	20.1
5	Memphis, Tenn.	19.4
6	San Antonio, Tex.	18.4
7	Houston, Tex.	17.6
8	Dallas, Tex.	17.5
9	Fresno, Calif.	17.2
10	Gary, Ind.	17.2
11	Miami–Dade, Fla.	17.0
	State of Florida	9.0

Rape

Rank	Location	Rape Rate per 100,000
1	St. Louis, Mo.	173.2
2	Tacoma, Wash.	106.4
3	Grand Rapids, Mich.	95.9
4	Jacksonville, Fla.	88.9
5	Memphis, Tenn.	82.8
6	Little Rock, Ark.	77.1
7	Nashville, Tenn.	74.2
8	Columbus, Ohio	71.0
9	Toledo, Ohio	70.2
10	Tucson, Ariz.	69.0
32	Miami–Dade, Fla.	54.2

Robbery

Rank	Location	Robbery Rate per 100,000
1	New York City	1237.1
2	Miami–Dade, Fla.	902.5
3	Los Angeles, Calif.	750.1
4	Baltimore, Md.	637.1
5	San Francisco, Calif.	578.1
6	Chicago, Ill.	577.4
7	New Orleans, La.	566.3
8	Memphis, Tenn.	539.5
9	Fresno, Calif.	478.1
10	Oakland, Calif.	452.8
	State of Florida	366.9

Aggravated Assault

Rank	Location	Assault Rate per 100,000
1	Miami–Dade, Fla.	1063.2
2	Los Angeles, Calif.	965.6
3	Little Rock, Ark.	959.7
4	Springfield, Mass.	954.0
5	Jacksonville, Fla.	916.7

(continued)

Aggravated Assault (*continued*)

Rank	Location	Assault Rate per 100,000
6	Tampa, Fla.	888.5
7	Albuquerque, N. Mex.	879.9
8	New York City	861.4
9	Charlotte, N.C.	817.3
10	Bakersfield, Calif.	787.7
	State of Florida	777.2

Property Crime

Rank	Location	Property Crime Rate per 100,000
1	Miami–Dade, Fla.	10,299.5
2	San Antonio, Tex.	8835.0
3	Palm Beach County, Fla.	7906.3
4	Jacksonville, Fla.	7728.6
5	Tucson, Ariz.	7678.1
6	Fresno, Calif.	7660.5
7	Austin, Tex.	7607.9
8	Broward County, Fla.	7547.4
9	Ft. Worth, Tex.	7491.8
10	El Paso, Tex.	7416.7
	State of Florida	7151.0

(*Source:* FBI, 1993.)

GETTING A GUN IN FLORIDA

On July 8, 1999, approval control numbers were issued by the Florida Department of Law Enforcement and a criminal background check was required. The permit is good for 30 days. Those denied a permit have 21 days to appeal. In 2000, the FDLE recorded 24,823 violent index crimes involving a firearm for the state. Almost 78% of all gun-related crime occurred in only ten counties: Broward, Miami–Dade, Duval, Hillsborough, Lee, Leon, Orange, Palm Beach, Pinellas, and Polk (see table).

FIREARM OFFENSE BY COUNTY

County	Robbery with Gun	Assault with Gun	Total Firearm Crimes
Broward	1108	828	1996
Miami–Dade	3037	2912	6147
Duval	979	1072	2117
Hillsborough	1319	937	2320
Lee	354	361	732
Leon	281	251	542
Orange	1012	863	1922
Palm Beach	763	803	1627
Pinellas	563	659	1255
Polk	50	354	624

CLASSIFYING TYPES OF CRIME

Each law enforcement agency is responsible for classifying crime that occurs within its jurisdiction. The agency is required to review the facts and determine the distinct offenses. Attempts to commit a crime are counted as if the crime was committed.

CRIME CLEARANCE RATES

The UCR collects data on crimes that have been cleared by the police. This is important data when used to measure productivity for police agencies. A common perception is that most crimes are cleared by arrest. Many investigations, however, determine that a crime never occurred; therefore, it is deleted. A crime is cleared by arrest when at least one person is arrested and charged with an offense related to the original crime. This could occur if a burglary was reported and a person was arrested but charged with trespassing. The police may indicate to the UCR that a Part I crime of burglary had occurred but was cleared by arrest. Also, in many cases, one arrest may clear several open investigations. Police may also clear cases by utilizing exceptional clearance criteria: when the police investigation has definitely established the identity of the offender and the police have enough information to support an arrest, when the police know the exact location of an offender, or when a reason beyond the control of law enforcement prevents the arrest and prosecution of the offender.

NATIONAL INCIDENT-BASED REPORTING SYSTEM

The law enforcement community realizes that it has the ability to collect and report more crime data. The complex contemporary society creates new and unique problems for police. Some complicated and multidimensional criminal acts and trends require a more detailed identification of crime. The Federal Bureau of Investigation (1998) published a preliminary view of a new reporting system that views a crime as an incident with components. To the FBI, each crime has eight elements:

1. Alcohol and drug influence
2. Specified location of the crime
3. Type of criminal activity involved
4. Type of weapon used
5. Type of victim
6. Relationship of victim to offender
7. Residency of victim and arrest
8. Description of property and their values

In addition, the National Incident-Based Reporting System (NIBRS) categorizes crime into 22 offenses, expanding from the traditional 8: murder, rape, robbery, assault, burglary, larceny, motor vehicle theft, and arson. The 22 offenses are:

1. Arson
2. Assault
3. Bribery
4. Burglary
5. Counterfeiting
6. Destruction of property
7. Drug offenses
8. Embezzlement
9. Extortion
10. Fraud
11. Gambling
12. Homicide
13. Kidnapping

14. Larceny

15. Motor vehicle theft

16. Pornography

17. Prostitution

18. Robbery

19. Sex offense (forcible)

20. Sex offense (nonforcible)

21. Stolen property

22. Weapons violation

FLORIDA CRIME VICTIMS' BILL OF RIGHTS

Under the State of Florida Crime Victims' Bill of Rights, victims of crime or their lawful representatives, including the next of kin of homicide victims, are entitled to the right to be informed, to be present, and to be heard, when relevant, at all crucial stages of criminal proceedings, to the extent that these rights do not interfere with the constitutional rights of the accused.

Constitution of the State of Florida, Article I, Section 16—Rights of Accused and Victims

(a) In all criminal prosecutions the accused shall, upon demand, be informed of the nature and cause of the accusation against him, and shall be furnished a copy of the charges, and shall have the right to have a compulsory process for witnesses, to confront at trial adverse witnesses, to be heard in person, by counsel or both, and to have a speedy and public trial by an impartial jury in the county where the crime was committed. If the county is not known, the indictment or information may charge venue in two or more counties conjunctively and proof that the crime was committed in that area shall be sufficient, but, before pleading, the accused may elect in which of those counties he will be tried. Venue for prosecution of crimes committed beyond the boundaries of the state shall be fixed by law.

(b) Victims of crime or their lawful representatives, including the next of kin of homicide victims, are entitled to the right to be informed, to be present, and to be heard when relevant, at all crucial stages of criminal proceedings, to the extent that these rights do not interfere with the constitutional rights of the accused.

Constitution of the State of Florida, Article 1, Section 16(B)—Victim Rights

Victims of crime have the right to:

- be treated with dignity and compassion

- be protected from intimidation and harm

- be informed about the availability of crime compensation and other victim services

- be informed about the criminal justice process

- submit a victim impact statement (if so desired)

- have property returned as quickly as possible

- seek restitution for loss of property and income, and seek reimbursement for medical expenses incurred as a result of the offense

- have restitution orders diligently and fairly enforced

Surviving family member of a victim whose death occurred as a result of a crime have all the same rights as listed above.

Victim/Witness Harassment

Interference with a victim or witness by threats or acts of revenge is a serious crime in itself and a matter to which the local police agency, the State's Attorney Office, and the court will give particular attention. If a victim or witness or his family is in any way threatened, immediate notification to the police or sheriff's office is required to ensure proper law enforcement action.

THE CRIMINAL JUSTICE PROCESS

The criminal justice process starts with the commission of a crime. The three basic methods by which a defendant may be brought to court are:

1. Arrest of the accused at the scene of the crime

2. Arrest based on a warrant issued by the court in response to a sworn complaint

3. Arrest based on an indictment by a grand jury as the result of an investigation

In all three instances, the evidence available must be sufficient to later convince the court that there is "probable cause" to believe that a crime was committed and that the person arrested took part in committing the crime. "Probable cause" means that there is reasonable belief that a crime has been committed.

Magistrate Hearing or First Appearance

Within 24 hours of the arrest, the defendant may appear before a judge for a magistrate hearing. At the magistrate hearing, the judge will set the conditions, if any, for release of the defendant from jail. When a person who is accused of a crime has sufficient roots in a community to ensure that the person will return for trial, the judge may release the accused on his own recognizance pending judicial proceedings. This means the accused does not have to post bond but promises to appear at a later date set by the court. Some defendants can post bond prior to the hearing, based on certain conditions. Some counties have a "no bond" policy for arrests relating to domestic violence acts. Most offices of the state's attorneys also have a policy of not dropping a criminal charge for domestic violence cases. Defendants may be prosecuted for domestic violence crimes without the victim. Victims and witnesses are not required to be present at this hearing but they have the right to attend and to make the judge aware of their feelings about the release of the accused. Victims can speak to an assistant state's attorney; however, they must indicate that desire to the county deputy or the victim/witness advocate in the magistrate room.

Bond Hearing

For many crimes, bail bonds have been previously determined by the courts and are contained in a list of standard bond amounts. This is a list of charges that have corresponding bail amounts; usually, the more serious the crime, the higher the bail. If the defendant is unable to post the standard bond amount or if the crime for which the accused has been arrested, such as murder, rape, robbery, or kidnapping, is not included in the standard bond list, the defendant will go to a first appearance hearing within 24 hours after arrest. This is called a *magistrate hearing* or *first appearance.*

Arraignment

An arraignment is the initial court appearance of the defendant at which time the court will inform the defendant of the charges pending, give the defendant his rights, appoint a lawyer if necessary, and hear the plea of the defendant. The two types of arraignment hearings are misdemeanor or felony arraignments:

- Misdemeanor crimes are punishable up to one year in jail.

- Felony crimes are punishable one year or longer in state prison.

These arraignments are set before a judge when a defendant is charged with an offense. At the arraignment, the defendant is told the nature of the charges and the possible penalties for the offense. The defendant may plead guilty and receive sentencing at this time or in some cases postpone for a sentencing date. At the arraignment, the defendant's ability to obtain an attorney is also assessed, and a public defender or attorney from a volunteer list may be appointed if he cannot afford a private attorney. Victims have a right to attend this hearing and address the court with their concerns.

Subpoena

A subpoena is a court order that requires a person and/or records to appear at a time, date, and place as indicated. Victims and witnesses may receive subpoenas for certain hearings and the trial. The telephone number of the victim/witness liaison should be on the subpoena. Victims and witnesses are required to call the liaison to receive instructions and/or changes regarding the court date or case status. Most cases do not go to trial; it is estimated that approximately 80% of criminal cases are deposed before trial. The State's Attorney Office will notify victims of various hearings, developments, and outcomes of the criminal process.

State's Attorney Investigation

Sometime after the magistrate hearing and before the arraignment, victims and witnesses may be notified to appear at the State's Attorney Office to give sworn statements regarding the crime. Because a crime is an offense against the State of Florida, the case against the accused may proceed with or without the victim's cooperation.

Information/No Information Filed

After statements are taken and an investigation conducted, the State's Attorney Office will make a determination based upon the facts presented as to the appropriate action. The state's attorney office may file an *Information,* a formal document filed with the clerk's office stating the charge(s) filed against the defendant. Also, the State's Attorney Office may file a *No-Information,* a formal document stating that the facts and circumstances as presented do not warrant prosecution at this time.

Impact Statement

A victim may file an impact statement with the State's Attorney at any time before a sentence is imposed on the defendant. The victim impact statement is a written or oral statement given by the victim describing the effect the crime has had on him and the losses suffered. The victim impact statement also advises the court of the victim's concerns or opinions in regard to the sentence. The opportunity to provide a victim impact statement may be obtained from the State's Attorney Office Victim Advocate Unit. This unit may also assist in completion of the form. The completed form will then be placed in the court file to be presented to the judge for consideration. Additionally, the victim may be present in Court to testify directly, in terms of suffering, financial loss, and other distress due to the crime.

Deposition

The attorney for the defendant can have a subpoena issued requiring victims or witnesses to appear and answer questions under oath concerning their knowledge of the criminal offense. This proceeding, where testimony is given, is referred to as a *deposition.* An assistant state's attorney can be present if requested in advance by the victim.

Pretrial Intervention

Pretrial intervention is a program designed for first-time offenders. The defendant must have the approval of the State's Attorney and the victim for acceptance into this program. If the defendant successfully completes the program, the criminal charges will be dropped. If the defendant fails to meet the terms of the program, the charges will be reactivated, and full prosecution will be pursued. Only nonviolent crimes are accepted into this program.

Status Conference

A status conference is a court proceeding in which the prosecuting and defense attorneys discuss the situation of the case. Certain motions concerning legal issues may be heard at the status conference. At this time the court is informed of a possible plea agreement or the availability of victims or witnesses for trial if a plea agreement cannot be reached. In addition, if the defendant, state, or court is not ready for trial and plea agreement cannot be reached, the judge will grant a continuance of the case. If the state and the defense cannot agree to a plea and a continuance is not granted by the judge, then the case will be scheduled for trial. If the defendant pleads guilty at this time, sentence may be imposed at the time of the plea or a sentencing date will be scheduled. Victims may appear at the sentencing hearing.

Continuances and Postponements

Florida courts are seriously overcrowded. Delays are often caused when various court proceedings are continued for any number of reasons. The State's Attorney or defendant's attorney may request a continuance in order to conduct further investigations of the case for other legal reasons. Many times these continuances may cause unnecessary trips to court for the victim. In cases where the victim or witness must take time off from work to assist in investigations, the investigating police agency, Victim Advocate Unit, or State's Attorney will assist in explaining circumstances to the victim's employers or creditors, if requested.

The Pre-Sentence Investigation

In a significant number of cases, pre-sentence investigations are conducted. The pre-sentence investigation consists of an interview with the defendant, a review of his criminal record, and a review of the specific facts of the crime. The probation department then makes a recommendation to the judge about the type and severity of the sentence.

The Trial

At the trial, the judge or a jury of citizens will decide whether the defendant is guilty or not guilty. First, the state will present its evidence, which may include the victim's testimony, then the defense will present its evidence. Attorneys for each side will have a chance to ask questions of every witness.

The Use of Peremptory Challenges

The U.S. Supreme Court has mandated that juries should be selected from a cross-section of the community, thus some jurors may be dismissed from the case. During the potential jury interviews, prosecutors and defense attorneys can use *peremptory challenges,* which means that a juror can be dismissed without reason or explanation; however, most challenges are used when either the prosecutor or the defense attorney gets an indication that the juror strongly opposes the desired point of view.

Sentencing

Many times sentencing of a defendant who pleads guilty or is found guilty takes place at the status conference or trial proceeding. If it is determined that sentencing will occur at a later time, the victim will receive notification of the scheduled date. Because sentencing can occur at any step, it is important to have the victim impact statement form completed and returned to the State's Attorney Office as soon as possible.

Return of Property

All property will be promptly returned to the victim or witness upon approval from the case filing agency, unless there is a compelling law enforcement reason for not returning it.

Appeals

Victims can be kept informed of any appeals by writing: Attorney General, Bureau of Crime Victims' Rights, The Capitol, Tallahassee, Florida 32399-1050 (telephone, 904-488-0600).

Prison

After a defendant is sent to prison, victims can be kept informed of the defendant's status by writing the Department of Corrections, 2501 Blairstone Road, Tallahassee, Florida 32399-2500, Attn.: Victim Assistance (telephone, 904-488-9166).

Crime Compensation

If someone is physically injured as a result of a crime, that individual may be eligible for monetary reimbursement of medical bills incurred and loss of wages through the Bureau of Crimes Compensation Program. The purpose of the program is to provide compensation to innocent victims of crimes or their families who suffer physical injury or death as a direct result of a crime. This is different from restitution paid by the defendant. In order to apply for Crimes Compensation, Victims Services should be contacted for further assistance. These forms are also available through hospitals, police departments, the State's Attorney Office, and sheriffs' offices.

Restitution

In addition to any punishment, the court will order the defendant to make restitution to the victim for damage or loss caused directly or indirectly by the defendant's offense. Restitution may be monetary or non-monetary. The State's Attorney has the responsibility to present to the court the dollar amount and items to be considered in any restitution hearing. For this reason, the victim impact statement must be filled out and documentation supplied to the Assistant State's Attorney handling the case at the earliest possible time. After an inmate's release, questions about restitution can be asked of the probation department.

Release of Defendant

When a term of imprisonment or involuntary commitment is imposed, the defendant may be released from such imprisonment or commitment by expiration of sentence or probation. Victims should be notified of any pending release of the sentenced defendant from a jail facility providing the victim's current home address is on file with the Victim Notification Unit.

Victim/Witness Assistance

Upon request from the victim or witness, assistance can be provided for such services as transportation, parking, separate pretrial waiting areas, and translator services for attending court, as is practical. Crime victims can obtain further information concerning these services by contacting the State's Attorney Office, Victim Advocate Unit, or Division of Victim Services.

Victim Services

The Florida Attorney General's Division of Victim Services not only serves as an advocate for crime victims and victims' rights but also administers a compensation program to ensure financial assistance for innocent victims of crime. As part of its responsibility, the division notifies victims of the status of any appellate decisions regarding their cases. Injured crime victims may be eligible for financial assistance for medical care, lost income, mental health services, funeral expenses, and other out-of-pocket expenses directly related to the injury. If needed, victims can also be referred to support organizations within their home area. In order to apply for assistance, check on the status of applications, or to seek any other assistance, this division should be contacted toll free from anywhere in the United States at 1-800-226-6667. (Tallahassee-area residents, 487-7015). In addition, victims may also contact the Division of Victim Services at 904-488-0848.

Victims of Domestic Assault

Domestic violence is defined as any assault, battery, sexual assault, sexual battery, or any crime that could result in death or injury to a family or household member by another. A family or household member is defined as a spouse, former spouse, persons related by blood or marriage, persons who are presently residing together or in the past have resided together like a family, and persons who have a child in common, regardless of whether they have been married or have resided together in the past.

Responsibilities of the Police

Florida State Statute 741.29 requires the police to investigate incidents of domestic violence:

- The police are obligated to make a written report whenever they respond to an alleged incident of domestic violence.

- Reports must include a description of any injuries observed.

- The report must include a narrative description of the events that allegedly occurred.

- If no arrest is made, the report must indicate why no arrest was made.

- Once dispatched, the police evaluate the situation. If evidence supports probable cause that an assault has occurred, an arrest is made. The victim should be advised of his or her rights and remedies under the law, provided information on safe-place shelters, and given the procedure for an injunction or protective order.

Injunction for Protection of Domestic Violence

Florida law provides protection from abuse or threats of violence from a spouse, former spouse, or another family member who is or was living in the same household. Marriage is not necessary for protection under the law. A person may petition for an order from the court prohibiting further contact and/or abuse. This document is commonly referred to as an *injunction*. The two types of domestic injunctions are:

1. *Temporary injunction,* which stands for a stated period of time not to exceed 30 days. Usually this type of injunction is given to a victim who is in immediate danger of physical abuse.

2. *Permanent injunction,* which stands for a period not to exceed one year unless extended by the court. A permanent injunction requires a court hearing.

Obtaining an Injunction

Most counties provide a facility usually associated with a courthouse for victims of domestic violence to process a petition for an injunction. The court clerk will usually assist a victim in completing the proper forms and associated documents. Injunctions may include the following:

- The person who abused or threatened the victim is ordered not to commit any acts of violence against anyone living in the household.

- The abuser must immediately leave the dwelling.

- The abuser (if not living with the victim) must stay away from the dwelling.

- Temporary custody of any children is granted.

- Counseling is provided for the abuser.

Violation of an Injunction

Florida State Statute 741.31 provides the following as violations of an injunction as a first-degree misdemeanor:

- refusing to vacate the dwelling or property that the parties share

- returning to the dwelling or property that the parties share

- committing an act of domestic violence against the petitioner

- committing any other violation of the injunction through an intentional unlawful threat, word, or act to do violence to the petitioner, coupled with an apparent ability to do so, and through some act that creates a well-founded fear that such violence is imminent

Domestic Violence Centers   Victims of domestic assault can obtain information and advice from police departments, sheriffs' offices, and state law enforcement agencies. Additionally, the table lists telephone numbers for assistance.

Location	Contact Number	Location	Contact Number
Bartow	813-533-3141	Naples	813-775-2011
Bradenton	813-747-7790	Ocala	904-622-8495
Bunnell	407-957-4673	Okeechobee	813-763-0202
Clearwater	813-442-4128	Orlando	407-886-2856
Cocoa	407-631-2764	Orange Park	904-284-0061
Dade City	904-567-1553	Panama City	904-763-0706
Daytona Beach	904-255-2102	Pensacola	904-434-6600
Delray Beach	407-265-2900	Port Charlotte	813-627-6000
Fort Lauderdale	305-761-1133	Port Richey	813-856-5797
Fort Myers	813-939-3112	Punta Gorda	813-627-0000
Gainesville	904-377-8255	Sarasota	813-365-1976
Inverness	904-344-8111	St. Petersburg	813-898-3671
Jacksonville	904-354-3114	Tallahassee	904-681-2111
Key West	305-294-0824	Tampa	813-247-7233
Key Largo	305-852-6222	Vero Beach	407-562-3374
Kissimmee	407-847-8562	St. Lucie County	407-464-4555
Marathon	305-743-4440	Martin County	407-288-7023
Miami (Safespace N.)	305-758-2546	West Palm Beach	407-655-6106
Miami (Safespace S.)	305-247-4249		

(*Source:* Florida State's Attorney's Office.)

CONCLUSION

A crime is the commission of an act in violation of law. Felonies and misdemeanors are the two general categories of crime in Florida. The *Florida Law Enforcement Handbook* defines a felony as any criminal offense that is punishable under the laws of this state, or that would be punishable if committed in its state, by death or imprisonment in a state penitentiary. A misdemeanor is any criminal offense that is punishable under the laws of this state, or that would be punishable if committed in this state, by a term of imprisonment in a county correctional facility, except for an extended term, not in excess of one year. The five categories of felonies are capital, life, first-degree, second-degree, and third-degree. Misdemeanors are categorized as first- or second-degree.

Crime is counted by two major sources: the *Uniform Crime Report* (UCR) and the *National Crime Survey* (NCS). The two means of reporting crime allow us to understand the crime index and crime rates. High crime rates in Florida can be accredited to various reasons such as drugs, guns, prison, the elderly, weather, diversity of class, and ethnic diversity. It should be noted that approximately 37% of all personal and household crimes are reported to the police. A plethora of reasons exist for citizens not reporting crimes. Victims of domestic violence are provided avenues of protection within the criminal justice system in Florida, ranging from shelters to injunctions. Additionally, the police role in domestic violence matters is changing due to national visibility and social priorities.

DISCUSSION QUESTIONS

1. Distinguish between a felony and a misdemeanor.

2. Compare and contrast the *Uniform Crime Report* and the *National Crime Survey*.

3. What are Florida's crime index offenses?

4. Identify five contributing factors to crime in Florida.

5. Discuss the role of the police officer at the scene of a domestic violence incident.

REFERENCES

Bureau of Justice Statistics. 1998. *Criminal Victimization 1990*. Washington, D.C.: U.S. Government Printing Office.

Edwards, S. M. 1989. *Policing 'Domestic' Violence: Women, the Law and the State*. Newbury Park, Calif.: Sage Publications.

Federal Bureau of Investigation (FBI). 1988. *Uniform Crime Reporting: National Incident-Based Reporting System*, Vol. 1, *Data Collection Guidelines*. Washington, D.C.: Federal Bureau of Investigation.

Federal Bureau of Investigation (FBI). 1990. *Crime in the United States: Uniform Crime Reports*. Washington, D.C.: Federal Bureau of Investigation.

Federal Bureau of Investigation (FBI). 1993. *Crime in the United States: Uniform Crime Report*. Washington, D.C.: Federal Bureau of Investigation.

Federal Bureau of Investigation (FBI). 1998. *Crime in the United States: Uniform Crime Report*. Washington, D.C.: Federal Bureau of Investigation.

Florida Criminal Law and Motor Vehicle Handbook. 1996. Longwood, FL: Gould Publications.

Florida Department of Law Enforcement (FDLE). 2000. *Crime in Florida: Annual Report*. Tallahassee, Fla. Florida Department of Law Enforcement.

Florida Law Enforcement Handbook. 1999. Miami–Dade, Fla.: Miami–Dade Police Department.

National Crime Survey Report. 1990. Washington, D.C.: U.S. Government Printing Office.

New Uniform Crime Reporting Data Ahead of Schedule, FBI Says. 1990. *Criminal Justice Newsletter*, 21 (May), 2.

Walker, L. 1978. *The Battered Woman*. New York: Harper & Row.

CHAPTER 4

Florida Police Systems

CHAPTER OVERVIEW

In this chapter, we review police systems in Florida from various perspectives, such as the role of the police officer and related duties. Additionally, the various levels of law enforcement are addressed which consist of local/city, county, state, and federal agencies. An in-depth discussion of the specific number of officers employed throughout the state is provided, and fluctuations and inconsistency in coverage from county to county are considered.

Also discussed are four models employed by Florida's agencies: full-service, law-enforcement, civil–judicial, and correctional–judicial. These four models are reflected in Florida's vast array of agencies, ranging from Indian, railroad, and local departments to state and federal agencies.

THE POLICE IN FLORIDA

Florida is one of the fastest growing states in America (Bureau of Economic and Business Research, 1993). Currently, according to the Bureau of Economic and Business Research, University of Florida, law enforcement agencies in Florida are responsible for a population of almost 16,000,000, with an additional 31 million annual tourists. With this growth in population, police agencies have increased their personnel to new levels; currently, 32,818 law enforcement officers provide police services for the inhabitants of Florida. Law enforcement in Florida is large, decentralized, and complex. Although each level of law enforcement has the overall function of combating crime, a great diversity exists in methods, style, approach, and technique.

Uniformed police officers are the most visible portion of the entire police population in the State of Florida. They represent the majority of the police departments and perform the bulk of the everyday police services requested from the public.

Police have two primary functions in the State of Florida: to enforce the statutory laws and to provide service to the community. Police patrol (motorized or on foot) and other forms of patrol visibility provide a degree of security to the general public and may act as a deterrent to potential criminals. Patrol also distributes police throughout the jurisdictions which aids in providing rapid response to reported criminal activity and emergencies.

Currently, the basic purposes of patrol have not changed since inception of police in this country over 150 years ago: deterrence of crime, maintenance of a feeling of public security, and 24-hour availability for service to the community (Walker, 1992).

The police/population ratio published in the Federal Bureau of Investigation *Uniform Crime Report* indicates the number of police officers employed is in correlation to the jurisdiction's total population. The Police Executive Research Forum (1981) found an average of 6.48 officers per 1000 population in large cities; however, Florida cities vary greatly with regard to this general rule. Regardless, in most cases, it appears that the number of police employed has little relationship to the crime frequency, type, or rate.

COMPONENTS OF FLORIDA LAW ENFORCEMENT

Law enforcement services are provided by four levels in the State of Florida:

- Federal
- State
- County
- Local/city

Municipal/Local Police Departments

Approximately 12,288 independent local police agencies operate in the United States, consisting of about 460,000 police employees. About 91% of local/city police departments employ less than 50 officers (see table) (Walker, 1992).

LOCAL/CITY POLICE DEPARTMENTS

Number of Sworn Personnel	N	Percent (%)
1000 or more	38	.3
500–999	34	.3
250–499	81	.7
100–249	356	2.9
50–99	575	4.7
25–49	1495	12.2
10–24	3279	26.7
5–9	2910	23.7
2–4	2561	20.8
1	959	7.8

(*Source:* FDLE, 1993.)

Municipal/city police make up the largest population of law enforcement officers in the state. Over 289 independent police departments operate within Florida. The administrator (chief, director, etc.) of each local police agency is appointed by the city political system (commission, mayor, city manager). Each of the 67 counties contains numerous municipal police departments. Each local police department is limited in authority and responsibility to the geographic confines of its jurisdiction. Setting aside any unusual circumstances, one would not find a police officer from one jurisdiction performing law enforcement functions infringing on the property of another. City police perform a wide range of basic police services, including order maintenance, city ordinance enforcement, criminal apprehension, and mediation of other related social problems. Within Florida, the size of police departments varies greatly (see table). The City of Miami (Miami–Dade County) employs approximately 1062 officers; in contrast, the City of Oakland (Orange County) employs only three officers.

County	Number of Police Agencies	County	Number of Police Agencies
Alachua	10	Charlotte	2
Baker	1	Citrus	3
Bay	9	Clay	3
Bradford	2	Collier	2
Brevard	14	Columbia	2
Broward	29	Dade (Miami–Dade)	28
Calhoun	2	Desoto	2

(continued)

County	Number of Police Agencies	County	Number of Police Agencies
Dixie	2	Marion	4
Duval	6	Martin	4
Escambia	3	Monroe	2
Flagler	3	Nassau	2
Franklin	2	Okaloosa	6
Gadsden	4	Okeechobee	2
Gilchrist	1	Orange	12
Glades	1	Osceola	3
Gulf	2	Palm Beach	35
Hamilton	3	Pasco	5
Hardee	4	Pinellas	25
Hendry	2	Poke	15
Hernando	2	Putnam	3
Highlands	3	St. Johns	3
Hillsborough	6	St. Lucie	3
Holmes	2	Santa Rosa	3
Indian River	5	Sarasota	5
Jackson	4	Seminole	8
Jefferson	2	Sumter	6
Lafayette	1	Suwannee	1
Lake	13	Taylor	2
Lee	5	Union	1
Leon	5	Volusia	16
Levy	3	Wakulla	1
Liberty	1	Walton	2
Madison	2	Washinton	2
Manatee	6		

(*Source:* FDLE, 1993.)

County Sheriff's Departments

Approximately 3100 sheriff's departments operate in the country, and they employ approximately 204,000 persons (U.S. Department of Justice, 1990). Many sheriff's departments (about 66%) are small, employing less than 25 sworn officers (see table).

SHERIFF'S DEPARTMENTS

Number of Sworn Personnel	*N*	Percent (%)
1000 or more	12	.4
500–999	21	.7
250–499	64	2.1
100–249	191	6.2
50–99	295	9.5
25–49	522	16.9
10–24	953	30.8
5–9	684	22.1
2–4	335	10.8

(*Source:* U.S. Department of Justice, 1990.)

Brown (1978) developed a typology of four different models of the office of sheriff:

- Full-service model

- Law enforcement model

- Civil–judicial model

- Correctional–judicial model

The Full-Service Model   This type of sheriff's office assumes responsibility for the enforcement of law. Similar to the local police, this office employs patrol officers, conducts criminal investigations, and handles police-related functions. The judicial portion may include courthouse security, the serving of civil and criminal court orders, and court-related matters. The corrections service carries out the function of the county jails. This may require personnel to serve as correction officers, to transport prisoners, and to perform other matters involving the keeping of persons incarcerated at the county level (see Chapter 8).

The Law Enforcement Model   The sheriff's office under this model limits its involvement with the criminal justice system to police-related enforcement. It consists of road patrol, conducting criminal investigations, and other police matters. Most sheriffs' offices in Florida concentrate their enforcement efforts in unincorporated areas, areas that are not within the jurisdiction of any city. The duties of the court and corrections are assumed by separate, sometimes private, agencies.

The Civil–Judicial Model   This model of sheriff's office is concerned only with the courts. It may provide security for court-related facilities within the county jurisdiction, serve court orders, and perform tasks requested by the court. This model does not provide street patrol officers nor does it take responsibility for county jails.

The Correctional–Judicial Model   This type of office maintains the jails and correctional facilities within the jurisdiction of the county. It may provide correction officers and assume responsibility for securing inmates of the county system. Additionally, this office provides functions assigned by the court, including the serving of court orders and maintenance of order and security for court buildings.

The Florida Sheriff's Office

The State of Florida has 67 counties. Each county has a sheriff's law enforcement office whose jurisdiction is limited to the respective county. Due to the consolidation of Duval County, which reports as a city, Florida has a count of 66 county agencies. Although most states have sheriffs' offices, Florida is a full-service model. The sheriffs in the State of Florida are elected by the residents of their respective counties. The 67 county sheriffs' offices all operate under the full-service model. The size of each sheriff's office differs, and to some degree the number of personnel is related to the population of the county. The sheriff and deputies have jurisdiction throughout the county; however, most restrict their enforcement to areas not patrolled by local police.

As an elected official, the sheriff commands a great deal of influence in county politics. This authority is compounded by mandate in the constitution of the State of Florida, Article VII, Section 1(d), which states: "County Officers. There shall be elected by the electors of each county, for terms of four years, a sheriff, a property appraiser, a supervisor of elections, and a clerk of the circuit court."

The constitution of the State of Florida supplies the political strength of a county sheriff, and that strength is far greater than that of municipal police chiefs, whose positions could be eliminated at the will of city management.

Chapter 30 of the Florida Statute outlines the duties and requirements of all Florida sheriffs:

30.09	Qualifications of deputies
30.10	Place of office
30.11	Place of residence (sheriff and deputies)
30.15	Powers, duties, and obligations
30.24	Transportation of prisoners
30.46	Color of motor vehicles (green and white)

FLORIDA STATE LAW ENFORCEMENT

State law enforcement is relatively new in the policing field, unlike the sheriff's office, whose heritage can be traced to colonial America. One of the earliest forms of state police did not begin until about 1835 with the Texas Rangers (Smith, 1940).

The four state law enforcement agencies are Florida Department of Law Enforcement, Florida Highway Patrol, Florida Fish and Wildlife Commission, and the Division of Beverage. All have law enforcement authority throughout the entire State of Florida. The Florida Department of Law Enforcement is primarily concerned with criminal investigations in rural areas and assisting small police agencies in the investigations of serious crimes. The Florida Highway Patrol performs the more traditional role of law enforcement by patrolling the roadways, both rural and urban. The Florida Fish and Wildlife Commission is, for the most part, water based and deals with violations of freshwater fishing and hunting laws. The commission has responsibility for enforcement of saltwater fishing laws, as well as accidents, thefts, and crimes involving watercraft. The Division of Beverage is directly linked to alcohol-dispensing businesses and investigates complaints and violations of state-held liquor licenses.

FLORIDA DEPARTMENT OF LAW ENFORCEMENT

In 1967, the Florida legislature merged the responsibilities of several state criminal justice organizations into the Bureau of Law Enforcement. The state law enforcement agency started with 94 positions and one commissioner, who reported directly to the governor. In 1969, the legislature refined and restructured the Bureau as the Florida Department of Law Enforcement (FDLE). The agency is directed by a commissioner who is appointed by the governor with the approval of at least three members of the cabinet. Today, the 1500 employees are disbursed among seven divisions:

1. Office of the Executive Director

2. Division of Criminal Investigation

3. Office of Information Resource Management

4. Division of Local Law Enforcement Assistance

5. Division of Criminal Justice Information Systems

6. Division of Standards and Training

7. Division of Human Resources Development

Additionally, the Florida Department of Law Enforcement has statutory responsibilities to:

- administer the state's uniform crime report, including the collection and analysis of crime data

- provide state investigative assistance to local or city law enforcement agencies

- conduct or assist in major criminal investigations that include public corruption, organized crime, racketeering, and other crimes of a completed nature

- develop and regulate statewide law enforcement and corrections standards and training requirements

- operate the Florida Crime Information Center in Tallahassee which provides crime data and criminal intelligence

- effectively operate regional crime laboratories to assist other law enforcement organizations in criminal investigations

- provide protection for the governor and immediate family; agents from FDLE also provide protection for other dignitaries visiting the state

- establish and administer the Organized Crime Institute and the Executive Institute of Criminal Justice

(*Source*: FDLE, 1993.)

State of Florida Agencies	Number of Officers
Division of Beverage	165
Florida Department of Law Enforcement	378
Florida Game and Fish Commission	341
Florida Highway Patrol	1588
Florida Marine Patrol	360

(*Source:* FDLE, 1993.)

STATE POLICE V. HIGHWAY PATROL

The International Association of Chiefs of Police in 1975 categorized state law enforcement into two broad groups:

- *State police:* A state law enforcement agency with uniformed field patrol force that provides general full service policing, including criminal investigations, road patrol, and related service. For example, the New Jersey State Police not only provide road patrol throughout the state but also provide narcotic enforcement, corruption investigations, and criminalistic support and assistance in high-profile criminal investigations.

- *Highway patrol:* A state law enforcement agency that concentrates on traffic, vehicle accident investigation, and roadway law enforcement. Although the highway patrol has law enforcement authority throughout the state, it serves mostly in highway traffic related functions. For example, the Florida Highway Patrol provides traffic law enforcement on roadways that include, but are not limited to, the Florida Turnpike, I-95, I-75, and other major state highways.

FEDERAL LAW ENFORCEMENT IN FLORIDA

Federal law enforcement exists in every state, including Florida. It is difficult to determine how many of the estimated 70,000 federal law enforcement officers are assigned to the State of Florida. Regardless of their numbers, they have law enforcement authority throughout the nation. Most federal enforcement agencies have designated assignments. The categories include white-collar crime, crimes against banks, and organized crime investigated by the Federal Bureau of Investigation. Crimes involving narcotic violations, illegal narcotic manufacturing, and smuggling and trafficking of illegal drugs are investigated by agents from the Drug Enforcement Administration. The Border Patrol's primary responsibilities are protecting the entry points and dealing with various imports of cargo and in some cases illegal immigration. The U.S. Marshal's Office is charged with protection of federal courthouses, federal prisoner transportation, and some assignments with airline safety. Postal inspectors concentrate on investigating crimes against the U.S. Post Office and crimes utilizing the postal system.

Although federal officers have jurisdiction throughout the United States, their assignments seldom impede investigations conducted by the state or local agencies, mostly due to a division of offenses. This practice is illustrated by the assistance of local police after a bank robbery; however, the investigation is conducted by the Federal Bureau of Investigation.

Federal Agency	Number of Personnel
Federal Bureau of Investigation	20,000
Drug Enforcement Administration	5000
U.S. Marshal Service	20,000
U.S. Customs Service	15,000

AMERICAN INDIAN TRIBAL POLICE

In addition to the multitude of law enforcement agencies within the State of Florida, it also has two Indian Tribal Police Departments: the Miccosukee Police and the Seminole Police.

Indian Tribal Police	Number of Officers
Miccosukee	10
Seminole	44

The Indian Tribal Police have general law enforcement authority within the jurisdictional boundaries of their respective federal reservations. They perform common police functions, including criminal investigations, order maintenance, and service to the Indian community.

RAILROAD POLICE IN FLORIDA

Police services to the railroads in Florida are provided by a *parapublic* model of policing. Railroad Special Agents are private security employees with public police authority. This arrangement between public and private agencies dates back to the 1800s, when railroads serviced areas that had not developed public law enforcement. Many states, including Florida, passed railroad police acts that enabled private railroad companies to establish proprietary security forces, with full police power. The police employees of each railroad company in Florida, including Amtrak, CSX, and Florida East Coast, are paid from private corporate funds; however, Florida State Statute 354.01 authorizes broad law enforcement power. The 1975 Report of the Task Force of Private Security estimated that 3500 railroad police are employed nationally. Many agents hold several state commissions; therefore, it is difficult to estimate the number of railroad agents in service in Florida. The major railroad companies in Florida probably employ less than 30 special agents. Currently, railroad police do not report crime for the *Uniform Crime Report;* however, they do publish a *Monthly Statistical Report of Railroad Police Activities.*

The Police and Security Section of the Association of American Railroads has outlined the basic objectives for railroad police:

- protection of life and property

- prevention and suppression of crime

- investigation of criminal acts committed on or against the railroad, patrons, or employees

---

ADDITIONAL INFORMATION

Amtrak Corporate Headquarters
40 Massachusetts Avenue NE
Washington, D.C. 20001
Telephone 202-906-2236

CSX Transportation Company
Police and Special Services
500 Water Street
Jacksonville, FL 32202
Telephone 904-359-3608

Florida East Coast Railway
Police and Special Services
P.O. Box 600630
Miami Springs, FL 33266
Telephone 305-887-2672

(*Source:* Association of American Railroads, 1990.)

- arrest of criminal offenders

- supervision of conduct on railroad property

- performance of accidents, claims, and safety investigations

THE PUBLIC SCHOOL POLICE

Miami–Dade County in Florida has the fourth largest public school system police department in the country (see table). This agency provides background and employment investigations for all teachers, staff, and school bus drivers and investigates allegations of misconduct. This department also performs police and patrol duties on campuses. Serious criminal offense investigations are assisted by the appropriate jurisdictional police agency.

School District	No. of Schools	No. of Employees	No. of Students	No. of Police Personnel
New York	1069	100,000	1,000,000	3716
Los Angeles	870	56,000	792,239	360
Chicago	540	46,000	450,000	784
Dade/Miami	312	37,000	312,000	150

THE ISSUE OF POLICE CONSOLIDATION

Over the years, the effectiveness of police agencies across the United States has been questioned (Kelling et al., 1974), and increasingly law enforcement services are being held to the same standards of accountability as other services (Cuniff, 1984; Ostrom et al., 1977). This trend includes the State of Florida. Many Florida law enforcement agencies now compete with other public services for limited financial resources. The crime rate of Florida has remained at the forefront of public attention despite increases in police costs.

Proponents of consolidating some police agencies argue that the complexity of city jurisdictional lines, the rapidly growing state population, and the increasing sophistication of criminals clearly indicate a need for an alternative to the current delivery of police service. The multiplicity of police agencies often duplicate services and frequently overlap in their jurisdictions. This duplication has long been recognized as a source of inefficiency. The fragmented, small police agency may not be able to adjust to new types of criminal behavior. Complicated crimes and drug trafficking systems may be too taxing for smaller police departments.

Many researchers conclude that small municipal boundaries will soon become barriers to controlling crime. The following issues have emerged as concerns when dealing with crime in a small community:

- mobile crime labs that are beyond the budget of small agencies

- absence of centralized communications

- lack of specialized training (homicide investigation, child molestation, etc.)

- absence of criminal tracking and computerized records

- lack of capability to deal with sophisticated drug smuggling and organized crime

In most areas of operation, the Florida criminal justice system has experienced some degree of consolidation. The Florida courts have undergone extensive revision and consolidation, resulting in a four-level state system. In terms of corrections, small municipalities no longer operate jails but contract requirements from the county system. The small independent police department may have become a luxury that few communities can afford.

Supporters of the decentralized or independent police system insist that many small jurisdictions neither have the need nor the desire for certain types of services but would be forced to share the costs of such if consolidated.

THE ROLE OF POLICE

The role of the police in society is a complex one. The rich diversity of ethnic and economic backgrounds of the population of Florida houses a wide variety of perceptions about police. The American Bar Association *Standards Relating to the Urban Police Function* (1990) has identified 11 elements of the standard police role:

1. Identify criminal offenders and criminal activity and, where appropriate, to apprehend offenders and participate in subsequent court proceedings.

2. Reduce the opportunities for the commission of some crimes through preventive patrol and other measures.

3. Aid individuals who are in danger of physical harm.

4. Protect constitutional guarantees.

5. Facilitate the movement of people and vehicles.

6. Assist those who cannot care for themselves.

7. Resolve conflict.

8. Identify problems that are potentially serious law enforcement or governmental problems.

9. Create and maintain a feeling of security in the community.

10. Promote and preserve civil order.

11. Provide other services on an emergency basis.

ACCREDITATION

The early 1970s produced a process of ensuring that law enforcement agencies meet a minimum standard. This self-directed accreditation process is utilized in several professions, including law and medicine. Police departments that meet the standards set by the Commission on Accreditation for Law Enforcement Agencies (CALEA) receive recognition. The Commission, created in 1979, includes members from the International Association of Chiefs of Police, The National Sheriffs' Association, The National Association of Black Law Enforcement Executives, and the Police Executive Research Forum. The standards require validation in 900 specific topics in nine major areas. Law enforcement agencies that apply are required to have a written policy on use of force and use of deadly force, written rules and regulations, an affirmative action plan, and procedures for dealing with citizens' complaints. Several Florida law enforcement agencies have successfully completed full accreditation, and numerous others are currently under consideration (CALEA, 1988).

ETHICS IN CRIMINAL JUSTICE

Corruption and Misconduct

From its inception, the American criminal justice system has been permeated with corruption and officer misconduct. Officer misconduct has been well documented throughout the rich history of the criminal justice system in this country. In 1931, the Wickersham Commission published *Lawlessness in Law Enforcement,* alerting the public to improper police behavior and abusive investigation tactics. The report disclosed that police officers made false reports, were involved in torture to obtain confessions, and planted evidence. The 1973 Knapp Commission reported systematic corruption within the New York City Police Department. This misconduct was so pervasive that it required defining two categories of corruption: "meat eaters" and "grass eaters". Meat eaters were aggressive and misused police authority for personal gains by demanding money; grass eaters also accepted money but for the most part the offender solicited their inaction in law enforcement. Sherman (1974) suggested categorizing corruption by levels:

- *Type I: Rotten Apples and Rotten Pockets.* This type of organization has a few corrupt officers who use their position for personal gain. As these officers band together, they form rotten pockets.
- *Type II: Pervasive Unorganized Corruption.* In this type of organization, the majority of the personnel are corrupt but work independently from one another.
- *Type III: Pervasive Organized Corruption.* In this type of organization, the majority of the personnel are corrupt and working together in a systematic fashion.

The perception of justice or fairness is the single most important issue that affects the confidence of a community when dealing with the criminal justice system. Improving the confidence of the community in their law enforcement is based on the premise that people working within the system have a thorough understanding of ethics and the serious lasting ramifications of unethical behavior. Misconduct or unethical behavior, either real or perceived, on the part of employees of the system has led to public estrangement and in some cases ignited antagonism.

Historically, few agencies have attempted to incorporate police ethics as policy. Unfortunately, within the numerous law enforcement agencies existing in Florida, ethics development is delivered in a one-dimensional and piecemeal manner. In fact, individual agencies in Florida have significantly different philosophies and policies dealing with ethical behavior. The consequences of inconsistent or inadequately understood ethics policies of some police agencies adversely affect personnel working in the system. A serious challenge exists in the maintenance of a high level of integrity.

According to *Goodman's Enforcing Ethics* (1998), the following factors contribute to an officer's decision-making skills:

E, Environment

T, Training academy

H, Home life

I, Individual

C, Citizens

S, Stress

Ultimately, Goodman maintains, officers who abide by policies, procedures, and laws should be commended for upholding the ethical standards upon which the criminal justice profession is founded. Those who violate policies, procedures, and laws should be punished for such inappropriate actions unbecoming to an officer of the law. The public demands and deserves quality service; anything less is unacceptable.

Unfortunately, research suggests that police and correction officers' incarceration rates are at their highest. Some criminal justice personnel appear to be involved in far more than accepting a free meal. Behavior based on acceptable morals and ethics must be completely understood for it to be followed. The term *moral* means what is judged as good conduct; conversely, *immorality* is bad conduct. A moral person has the capacity to make value judgments and determine right from wrong.

Illegal and unethical acts by criminal justice personnel undermine the goals and objectives of the organization. This type of dangerous misconduct often arises from the frustrations of officers who perceive that the legal system is favoring the defendants. The planting of evidence, distortion of facts, false reports, and brutality emerge as attempts to balance the scales. Unethical conduct must be replaced with a uniform and unified belief in the rights of citizens and a level of professionalism unmatched by others.

The Florida Criminal Justice Standards and Training Commission

In 1967, the Florida Police Standards Council was established to address several problems with a lack of training and recruitment. This effort created a 12-member council with specific authorization to develop minimum standards and set criteria for training programs. In 1970, the Florida Police Standards Council was renamed the Florida Police Standards Board and placed under the Department of Community Affairs. In 1974, the legislature merged the Florida Police Standards Board and the Florida Department of Law Enforcement into one agency. The Florida Police Standards and Training Commission emerged as the organization that would set the conditions for training. The Commission provides statewide leadership, direction, and implementation and evaluation of standards in training for all law enforcement, correctional, and correction probation officers in Florida. In 1981, the legislature changed the name of the Florida Police Standards and Training Commission to the Criminal Justice Standards and Training Commission. Among some new additional duties, they were now required to hold meetings that were open to the general public.

Authority to Discipline   The Commission certifies and disciplines criminal justice officers in Florida, pursuant to Section 943.1395, F.S., which provides for Commission disciplinary action against an officer who fails to maintain minimum standards and good moral character. Failure to maintain good moral character is defined as behavior that would:

- Constitute a felony, whether criminally prosecuted or not

- Constitute a serious misdemeanor, whether criminal prosecuted or not

- Give rise to substantial doubts about an officer's respect for the rights of others or for the law

- Involve the use of controlled substances

The Commission can decertify an officer convicted of a felony offense or upon a pleading of *nolo contendere,* regardless of whether there is a withholding of adjudication. The officer's certificate may also be revoked if the officer is convicted of a misdemeanor of perjury or false statements. Revocation of certification is permanent and prohibits a person from criminal justice employment in the State of Florida.

The Disciplinary Process

- Individual agencies are required to report serious misconduct to the Commission.

- Case development and investigation are conducted.

- Case is presented to the Probable Cause Panel. If the Probable Cause Panel finds that the allegations are believed to be a serious violation, they are required to file a formal charge against the officer by issuing an Administrative Complaint that specifies the violation committed.

- Formal hearing is held. An Administrative Law Judge will hear testimony of witnesses and examine facts surrounding the violation. Upon conclusion, the Judge will forward to the Commission a recommendation of the finding of fact.

- Copies of the final orders of the Commission actions are forwarded to the officer and the employing agency.

AN OVERVIEW OF DISCIPLINARY ACTION

Commission Determination	Law Enforcement Officers	Correctional Officers	Total
Revocation	129	147	276
Suspension	9	7	16
Reprimand	3	2	5
Probation	83	62	145
No cause	18	20	38

(*Source:* Florida Police Standards and Training Commission to the Criminal Justice Standards and Training Commission, 1995.)

FREQUENTLY ASKED QUESTIONS

The role of contemporary police in society is complex. The rich diversity of ethnic and economic backgrounds creates a spectrum of individual perceptions. Police are one of the few social systems that provide service 24 hours per day. Police departments from Metro-Miami–Dade, Miami Beach, Fort Lauderdale, and Jacksonville have provided some frequently asked questions from the public.

- *How long will it take to get an officer here?* Police service calls are rated by priority, and arrival time depends on the seriousness of the call. A major consideration is the number of police units available. Every request for a police officer has a preprogrammed priority when it is routed to the dispatcher. If the circumstances change, the call can be upgraded to a higher priority.

- *Is your department/agency hiring now?* Most law enforcement agencies recommend that citizens interested in careers as police officers contact the Human Resource Department for that particular agency.

- *Why do you take some crime reports over the telephone instead of sending a police officer?* If, for example, a property crime is a larceny of a bicycle and there are no mitigating circumstances in progress, such as injuries or the description of offenders, the public may be better served if police officers remain available to respond to more serious crimes. Usually the telephone report center operator will obtain the same information that would have been obtained by an officer at the scene. Many minor traffic accidents can be handled with a Driver Exchange of Information form. The form is self-explanatory and prenumbered and has directions.

- *How can I get a tape made of my 911 call?* All police departments record conversations on emergency lines. For a processing fee, citizens can obtain a copy by contacting the records custodian with the time and date. Many police agencies may only keep tape recordings for 30 days.

- *A person was arrested by your police last night; where is he?* Depending on the charge, most people arrested by the police are transported to the county jail. A person booked into the county facility falls under county jurisdiction. All inquiries are made through the sheriffs' departments at the appropriate facilities.

- *How do I get a copy of a police report?* Police reports, including traffic accidents, are obtained from the Records Unit at the police agency that took the report. Most records are available between 9:00 a.m. and 5:00 p.m., Monday through Friday, and a fee per page is usually charged.

- *When can I make a missing person report and when will the police investigate?* If the missing person is a child the police will take immediate measures to report and investigate the matter. An adult without suspicious or mitigating circumstances may require 24 hours.

- *Can the police recommend an automobile repair shop?* The police department does not make recommendations for privately owned businesses. Agencies such as the Chamber of Commerce or Better Business Bureau should be contacted.

- *Can the police help me collect money due from a tenant?* No, most cities provide a landlord–tenant dispute center, or a complaint can be filed in small claims court at the county courthouse.

- *Can the police give me a name and address from a license plate number?* No; access to information from the police computer is for official use only. If the matter involves criminal and suspicious conduct, a police report will be taken.

CONCLUSION

Police have two primary functions in the State of Florida: enforce the statutory laws and provide service to the community. The basic purposes of patrol have not changed since the inception of police in the United States over 150 years ago: deterrence of crime, maintenance of a feeling of public security, and 24-hour availability for service to the community (Walker, 1992).

Over 289 independent local police agencies operate in the State of Florida, ranging from 3 officers in the City of Oakland to over 1000 in the City of Miami. Also, there are 67 sheriff's offices, 5 state law enforcement agencies, 4 federal agencies, 2 American Indian tribe police departments, a railroad police force, and public school police in Florida.

DISCUSSION QUESTIONS

1. Discuss police fragmentation in Florida.

2. Identify the 4 levels of law enforcement within the state.

3. Identify the 4 different models of the office of sheriff.

4. Explain the term *parapublic* and discuss railroad special agents.

5. Discuss the standards relating to the urban police function.

REFERENCES

American Bar Association (ABA). 1995. *Standards Relating to the Prosecution Function and Defense Function.* Washington, D.C.: American Bar Association.

Alpert, G. and R. Dunham. 1992. *Policing Urban America,* 2nd ed. Prospect Heights, Ill.: Waveland Press.

American Bar Association (ABA). 1990. *Standards Relating to the Urban Police Function.* Washington, D.C.: American Bar Association.

Association of American Railroads (AAR). 1990. *The Police Section.* Washington, D.C.: Association of American Railroads.

Brown, L. P. 1978. The role of the sheriff, in A. W. Cohn, ed., *The Future of Policing.* Beverly Hills, Calif.: Sage Books.

Bureau of Economic and Business Research. 1993. *Florida Statistical Abstract.* Gainesville, Fla.: University of Florida.

Champion, D. J. 1990. *Criminal Justice in the United States.* Columbus, Ohio: Merrill.

Commission on Accreditation for Law Enforcement Agencies (CALEA). 1988. *Standards.* Washington, D.C.: Commission on Accreditation for Law Enforcement Agencies.

Cuniff, M. 1984. *Beyond Crime: Law Enforcement Operational and Cost Data.* Washington, D.C.: National Association of Criminal Justice Planners.

Dade Circuit Court. 2000. Judge Scott Silverman, Miami Beach, Fla.

Dade County State's Attorney Office, Miami, Fla.

Ferdico, J. N. 1992. *Criminal Law and Justice Dictionary.* St. Paul, Minn.: West Publishing.

Ferdico, J. N. 1996. *Criminal Procedure for the Criminal Justice Professional,* 6th ed. St. Paul, Minn.: West Publishing.

Florida Department of Law Enforcement (FDLE). 1990–1993. *Crime in Florida: Annual Report.* Tallahassee, Fla.: Florida Department of Law Enforcement.

Florida Law Enforcement Handbook. 1996. Longwood, Fla.: Gould Publications.

Florida State Statutes. 1991. Special Officers for Carriers.

Goodman, D. 1998. *Enforcing Ethics.* Upper Saddle River, N.J.: Prentice Hall.

Hanley, J. R., W.W. Schmidt, and R. K. Robbins. 1991. *Introduction to Criminal Evidence and Court Procedure,* 2nd ed. Berkeley, Calif.: McCutchan Publishing.

Kelling, G. et al. 1974. *The Kansas City Preventive Patrol Experiment.* Washington, D.C.: The Police Foundation.

National Advisory Commission on Criminal Justice Standards and Goals. 1973. *Police.* Washington, D.C.: U.S. Government Printing Office.

Ostrom, E., R. B. Parks, and G. P. Whitaker. 1977. *Policing Metropolitan America.* Washington, D.C.: U.S. Government Printing Office.

Police Executive Research Forum. 1981. *A Model Policy Statement.* Washington, D.C.

Senna, J. J. and L. J. Siegel. 1990. *Introduction to Criminal Justice,* 5th ed. St. Paul, Minn.: West Publishing.

Sherman, L. W. (1974). *Police Corruption: A Perspective on Its Nature and Control.* Washington, D.C.

Smith, B. 1940. *Police Systems in the United States.* New York: Harper & Brothers.

Swanson, C. R., L. Territo, and R. W. Taylor. 1993. *Police Administration: Structures, Processes, and Behavior,* 3rd ed. New York: Macmillian.

Timm, H. and K. Christian. 1991. *Introduction to Private Security.* Belmont, Calif.: Wadsworth.

Travis, T. F. III. 1990. *Introduction to Criminal Justice.* Cincinnati, Ohio: Anderson Publishing.

U.S. Department of Justice. 1990. *Profile of State and Local Law Enforcement Agencies.* Washington, D.C.: U.S. Government Printing Office.

Walker, S. 1992. *The Police in America: An Introduction,* 2nd ed. New York: McGraw-Hill.

Wycoff, M. A. 1982. *The Role of the Municipal Police: Research as a Prelude to Changing It.* Washington, D.C.: Police Foundation.

Miami–Dade Police Department Performance Improvement Continuum

Effective Strategies for Police Performance Improvement and Community Partnership within a Dynamic and Complex Multicultural Environment

Leading and managing change in a complex and demanding police environment is often viewed as both a difficult and challenging process. Without an established model or framework to guide their actions, police chiefs are often forced to rely on the goals and objectives of the previous administration, thereby limiting their options or possibilities. At times, police chiefs base their strategies and make day-to-day decisions based solely on past practices as well as the working philosophy of the previous administration. Although this approach may present a solution for immediate problems and perhaps temporarily avoid conflict within the organization, it limits the type of strategic thinking necessary for continuous organizational growth and improvement.

Under the leadership of Director Carlos Alvarez, the Miami–Dade Police Department has chosen to deviate from a leadership style using exclusively a past practice approach to creating a policing model that focuses on implementing effective innovative strategies for police performance improvement through strong community partnerships. The main objective of the Miami–Dade Police Department Performance Improvement Continuum (see figure) is to develop and implement effective strategies to reduce crime and focus on quality-of-life issues, in order to enhance trust and confidence in the police from all its stakeholders.

The main components of this model include the following:

- Leadership
  - ➤ A personalized Mission Statement that is institutionalized within the organizational framework
  - ➤ Promotional appointments that are consistent with the leader's philosophy
  - ➤ Ability to build relationships with local government and all its stakeholders
  - ➤ An innovative vision for change
  - ➤ Succession planning and employee development
  - ➤ Ability to balance enforcement and service

- Community Relations
  - ➤ Community Policing Philosophy instilled in all uniformed personnel
  - ➤ Mandatory community board meetings by all district stations to establish strong community partnerships

- Governmental Support Liaison
  - ➤ Animal Control

Miami–Dade Police Department
Performance Improvement Continuum

> Effective strategies for police performance improvement and community partnership within a dynamic and complex multicultural environment

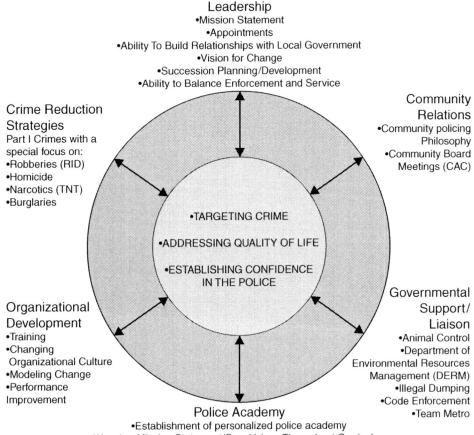

Leadership
•Mission Statement
•Appointments
•Ability To Build Relationships with Local Government
•Vision for Change
•Succession Planning/Development
•Ability to Balance Enforcement and Service

Crime Reduction Strategies
Part I Crimes with a special focus on:
•Robberies (RID)
•Homicide
•Narcotics (TNT)
•Burglaries

Community Relations
•Community policing Philosophy
•Community Board Meetings (CAC)

•TARGETING CRIME

•ADDRESSING QUALITY OF LIFE

•ESTABLISHING CONFIDENCE IN THE POLICE

Organizational Development
•Training
•Changing Organizational Culture
•Modeling Change
•Performance Improvement

Governmental Support/ Liaison
•Animal Control
•Department of Environmental Resources Management (DERM)
•Illegal Dumping
•Code Enforcement
•Team Metro

Police Academy
•Establishment of personalized police academy
•Weaving Mission Statement/Core Values Throughout Curriculum
•From an Exclusively Military Model to a Service-Oriented Model
•Personnel Hand-Picked Based on Education, Background, and Credentials

> Department of Environmental Resources Management (DERM)

> Illegal Dumping

> Code Enforcement

> Team Metro

> Quality-of-life issues with the citizens of Miami–Dade County

• Police Academy

> The Miami–Dade Police Department administers its own Police Academy for the purpose of institutionalizing their mission and philosophy of policing to all its trainees.

> The Mission Statement and Core Values of the Department are woven throughout the Police Academy curriculum.

> The methodology of the instruction has changed from an exclusive military model to a service-oriented model of policing.

➤ The leadership and personnel of the Police Academy have been selected based on education, police experience, and overall training credentials.

- Organizational Development

  ➤ Training

  ➤ Changing the organizational culture

  ➤ Focus on modeling the desired change

  ➤ Focus on performance improvement

- Crime Reduction Strategies

  ➤ Part I crimes concentrating on minimizing the impact of robberies, homicides, narcotics, and burglaries

CHAPTER 5

Prosecution and Defense

INTRODUCTION

This chapter presents an in-depth look at the prosecution and defense mechanisms within the State of Florida. Without an understanding of the legal role and responsibilities of both sides in a criminal case and the judicial process, justice for society and the defendant cannot be achieved. Initially, the role of the prosecution is discussed, followed by that of the defense. In order for both sides to be effective, each must fully understand the motivation of the other, as well as the roles of others involved in the judicial process such as the police, witnesses, and grand juries.

Once a criminal defendant has been processed by the police and evidence in the case has been gathered by police, the case is turned over to the prosecutor. It is the prosecutor's role to bring forward the state's case against the accused. The prosecutor has the authority to charge a person with a crime, release the individual from prosecution, or eventually bring the accused to trial. Whether or not to charge a person with a crime is at the discretion of the prosecutor.

The defense attorney works opposite the prosecutor in the criminal justice process. All defendants have a constitutional right (Sixth Amendment of the U.S. Constitution) to a defense attorney. Defendants may hire private defense attorneys of their choosing if they can afford to do so. If the accused cannot afford a defense attorney, and the state is seeking a jail or prison sentence, an attorney must be provided at the expense of the state (*Gideon v. Wainwright*, 1968, United States Supreme Court; *Argersinger v. Hamlin*, 1972, United States Supreme Court).

THE PROSECUTION

Types of Prosecutors

United States Attorney

United States attorneys for each judicial district are appointed by the President of the United States. The general responsibility of U.S. attorneys in the criminal justice system is to prosecute federal offenses.

State's Attorney

At the state and county level, the chief prosecutorial officers are the attorneys general and the state's attorneys. The Florida Attorney General is elected every 4 years by citizens in Florida. County State's Attorneys are elected every 4 years by citizens in their respective counties. The Florida constitution allows for one state's attorney for each of the 67 counties. The state's attorney provides personnel and procedures for orderly, efficient, and effective investigation, intake, and processing of all felony, misdemeanor, criminal traffic, juvenile, and specially enumerated civil cases referred by law enforcement; other state, county, and municipal agencies, and the general public.

Duties of the State's Attorney

The prosecutor has many responsibilities. From the time of arrest to final sentencing and appeals, the prosecutor participates in every phase of the criminal justice process. He or she enforces the laws, represents the government, and is the public spokesperson for the criminal justice system. The state's attorney is constitutionally charged with the duty to see that the laws of Florida are faithfully executed. The state's attorneys are the chief prosecuting officers for all trial courts in their judicial circuits. The state's attorneys, with the aid of appointed assistants (attorneys) and staff, appear in circuit and county courts within their judicial circuits and prosecute or defend on behalf of the State of Florida all suits, applications, or motions, civil and criminal, in which the State is a party. State's attorneys assist police in the investigation of crimes, interview (and subpoena when necessary) witnesses in criminal cases, and review applications for arrests and search warrants. The state's attorneys are required to represent the State in the prosecution of all criminal cases arising out of their respective circuits. A criminal case may be generated by several different events.

Arrest of an Offender

The state's attorney must review every arrest for violations of state law. This review process can be extensive. The state's attorney must rely on law enforcement to prepare arrest reports, victim affidavits, and witness statements and to secure the evidence needed to prove each and every element of the offenses charged. When law enforcement cannot provide this information, the state's attorneys obtain it through their investigative staffs. Once the state's attorney has reviewed all supporting documents and sworn testimony, a decision is made to file an *information* (a charge against the accused), decline to file any charges (dismiss the case), or require additional investigation. Upon the filing of an Information or indictment (charge), the case proceeds to arraignment, discovery preparation, pretrial hearings, trial or plea, and, finally, sentencing. The appellate process then begins. The state's attorney must respond if the appeal is from county court to circuit court and may respond to circuit court to district or supreme court.

Non-Arrest Walk-In Complaints

The state's attorney receives from various sources, including law enforcement and the general public, complaints and reports of criminal activity. Each one of these complaints must be investigated thoroughly to determine whether a crime has occurred and who has committed the crime. These investigations take place prior to the arrest of the accused. The investigation may include substantial witness statements, search warrants, subpoenas, and more. When the state's attorney has completed his or her investigation, with or without the assistance of law enforcement, a decision is made to either file an information or decline to file any charges. If charges are filed, an arrest warrant or summons must be prepared to bring the accused into custody. Once the accused is arrested, the case proceeds to arraignment, discovery preparation, motion response, pretrial hearings, trial, and sentencing. The appellate process then begins.

Investigations Initiated by State's Attorneys

The state's attorney office may initiate an investigation if it has reason to believe a crime has occurred and an investigation is warranted.

Executive Assignments

The state's attorney receives assignments to investigate and prosecute cases outside its jurisdiction when the governor's office assigns a case. This occurs when another circuit has a conflict and requests that the governor reassign the prosecution.

Grand Jury Investigations

The function of the grand jury in criminal matters is to investigate and determine whether sufficient evidence justifies an indictment against an accused. The grand jury must determine whether there is probable cause that a crime has been committed by the person accused. If they determine that the evidence is sufficient to constitute probable cause, they issue a *true bill,* which then becomes the indictment on which the accused will be brought to trial. The state's attorney must attend hearings of the grand jury for the purpose of examining witnesses in their presence, giving legal advice in any matter before them, and preparing of bills of indictment. Prosecutors are not required to obtain grand jury indictments (except in capital crimes) in order to bring someone to trial. The Florida constitution guarantees that "no person shall be tried for a capital crime without presentment or indictment by a Grand Jury" (Article I, Section 15a). Capital crimes are felonies for which the penalty is life imprisonment or death.

Statewide Prosecutor

The statewide prosecutor's office is responsible for investigating and prosecuting multicircuit organized crime throughout the State of Florida. Florida's transient population creates opportunities for crimes to be committed in various counties. For this reason, the office of the statewide prosecutor was created by amendment to the Florida constitution in 1986 to prosecute statewide cases. The statewide attorney is granted authority and jurisdiction from Article IV, Section 4, of the Florida constitution and Section 16.56 of the Florida statutes. The main offices of the statewide prosecutor are in Tampa, Hollywood, Orlando, Jacksonville, and Tallahassee. Statewide prosecutors handle crimes involving two or more judicial circuits, as well as criminal conspiracy in two or more judicial circuits, and have basically the same powers as state's attorneys. Additionally, cases prosecuted by the statewide prosecutor's office must fall within at least one of the following offenses:

1. Bribery
2. Burglary
3. Carjacking
4. Criminal fraud
5. Criminal usury
6. Extortion
7. Gambling
8. Home invasion robbery
9. Kidnapping
10. Larceny
11. Murder
12. Perjury
13. Prostitution
14. Robbery
15. Antitrust violations
16. Fencing violations
17. Narcotics violations
18. Racketeering violations

Cases are often referred to the statewide prosecutor's office from other police agencies. A statewide prosecutor usually has about ten active cases at a time (county state's attorneys can have hundreds). This is because statewide prosecutors are often involved in a case prior to an arrest. Statewide prosecutors assist police agencies in investigations to ensure that procedures are followed correctly and that they are gathering enough evidence to properly try cases. They also serve as the legal advisor to the statewide grand jury, whose function is to investigate and issue findings of fact, through the return of indictments or presentations, regarding organized criminal activity which has significance in more than one judicial circuit.

The Relationship Between Prosecutors and the Police

Prosecutors have an important function in their dealings with the police. Prosecutors rely on police personnel to initiate complaints against individuals for crimes. In more serious offenses, prosecutors are often involved in the investigative stage of a case (prior to an arrest). Deciding whether or not to prosecute and how to prosecute are the ultimate decisions made by the prosecutor.

Organized Crime Investigators

Organized crime investigators are police officers (county, municipal, or sheriff's deputies) assigned by the state's attorney office (with the consent of the county, municipality, or sheriff) to serve on a special task force to investigate matters involving organized crime. They have full arrest powers in accordance with the laws of the State of Florida.

Prosecutorial Discretion

As mentioned earlier, it is at the discretion of the prosecutor whether or not to charge a person with a crime. The prosecutor must determine the probability of each case resulting in a conviction at trial. A substantial portion of criminal defendants are never brought to trial. Even when the prosecutor initially decides to pursue a case, the charges may be dropped later in a process called *nolle prosequi*.

Just as police do not arrest for every minor violation of the law (jaywalking, for example), prosecutors do not prosecute every case that comes to them. If prosecutors were forced to prosecute each and every case brought before them, it has been said that the criminal justice system would become inoperable. This is because the criminal justice system is not designed to accommodate as many cases as are referred to the prosecutor's office. Prosecutorial discretion, when exercised properly, is an advantage of the criminal justice system. Discretion ensures that criminal laws will not be implemented in an unnecessarily rigid fashion.

In more serious felony cases, the state's attorney often seeks an *indictment* from a grand jury in deciding whether or not to prosecute a case. This usually involves a hearing where the grand jury, usually members of the community, hear evidence and decide whether or not there is enough evidence to proceed with the case. The state's attorney is not, however, required to get an indictment from a grand jury to prosecute, unless the accused will be charged with a capital offense. This is at the discretion of the state's attorney.

Due to the high volume of criminal cases, some cases must be diverted away from the criminal courts. This is done through various diversion programs offered to some criminal defendants (usually first-time offenders) prior to trial. Diversion programs allow a defendant to attend a treatment program or perform community service. Upon completion of the program, the charges are dropped. This gives the defendant a lighter penalty and relieves the court system of excess cases. This procedure also ensures that such defendants will not have a conviction on their criminal records. One of the most common reasons for dismissal of a criminal case is insufficient physical evidence linking a defendant to the crime. Another reason a case may be dismissed is that the prosecutor is having trouble with witnesses, such as witnesses failing to appear, giving unclear and inconsistent testimony, or recanting previous testimony. A case may also be dismissed because the defendant has agreed to plead guilty to a more serious offense. The American

Bar Association provides guidelines for prosecutorial discretion in its *Standards Relating to the Prosecution Function and Defense Function:*

A. In addressing himself to the decision whether to charge a defendant, the prosecutor should first determine whether there is evidence that would support a conviction.

B. The prosecutor is not obliged to present all charges that the evidence might support. The prosecutor may in some circumstances, and for good cause consistent with the public interest, decline to prosecute, notwithstanding that evidence exists that would support a conviction. Illustrative of the factors that the prosecutor may properly consider in exercising his or her discretion are:

   1. prosecutor's reasonable doubt that the accused is in fact guilty

   2. extent of harm caused by the offense

   3. disproportion of the authorized punishment in relation to the particular offense or the other offender

   4. possible improper motives of a complainant

   5. prolonged nonenforcement of a statute, with community acquiescence

   6. reluctance of the victim to testify

   7. cooperation of the accused in apprehension or conviction of others

   8. availability and likelihood of prosecution by another jurisdiction

C. In making the decision to prosecute, the prosecutor should give no weight to the personal or political advantages or disadvantages that might be involved or to a desire to enhance his record of convictions.

D. In cases that involve a serious threat to the community, the prosecutor should not be deterred from prosecution by the fact that in his jurisdiction juries have tended to acquit persons accused of the particular kind of criminal act in question.

E. The prosecutor should not bring or seek charges greater in number or degree than he can reasonably support with evidence at trial.

Prosecutors are officers of the court and, as such, are required to uphold the integrity of the criminal justice process. While it is the primary responsibility of prosecutors to enforce laws, it is their secondary (and perhaps most important) responsibility to ensure that justice is done. If a prosecutor discovers evidence that suggests that the accused is innocent, the prosecutor must inform the court of this fact, even though it would result in a loss for the prosecution. Oftentimes, prosecutors face pressure from their supervisors and the public to obtain a guilty verdict. Prosecutors must balance this pressure with the ethical responsibility of ensuring that innocent people are not punished.

THE DEFENSE

Public Defenders

Just as Florida has an elected chief prosecuting officer, it also has a chief public defender who is elected for a term of 4 years. Each judicial circuit has one elected public defender. The public defender must be a member, in good standing, of the Florida Bar for the preceding 5 years. The public defenders appoint assistant public defenders (attorneys) who work for them.

Duties of the Public Defender

Public defenders represent defendants who have been found by the court to be *indigent* and are charged with a felony, misdemeanor punishable by imprisonment, or criminal contempt, unless the court, prior to trial, files a statement that the defendant will not be imprisoned if convicted. In addition, public defenders represent juveniles at delinquency hearings and people for whom involuntary placement in residential service facilities for the mentally ill is being sought. Public defenders may not, under any circumstances, be appointed to represent any person who is not indigent.

Determination of Indigency

In order for an accused individual to have a public defender appointed to represent him or her, the accused must be found by the court to be indigent. The accused must file an affidavit with the court that he or she is unable to pay for the services of an attorney, including costs of investigation, without substantial hardship to the person or his or her family. If the defendant has been released on bail of more than $5000, has no dependents, has a weekly income that exceeds $100 (if he or she has dependents, the accused's weekly income must exceed $100 plus $20 for each of the first two dependents and $10 for each additional dependent), and has more than $500 in cash, the defendant is not entitled to the services of a public defender (Miami–Dade County State's Attorney Office, 1998).

The Role of the Defense Attorney

The defense attorney has many functions and responsibilities in his or her representation of a criminal defendant. A defense attorney will interview the defendant, the police, and witnesses, in addition to investigating the alleged crime and meeting with the prosecutor to discuss the case. The defense attorney represents the defendant at various stages of the criminal justice process, usually just after arrest, at pretrial hearings, and during questioning by police, arraignment, and trial. The defense attorney also enters into plea bargaining negotiations with the prosecution. In addition, the defense attorney represents the accused during trial, sentencing, appeals, and often through release from the criminal justice system.

The Pretrial Deposition

In 1968, the Florida Supreme Court created a system that permits sworn statements to be taken from witnesses, police officers, and victims in criminal cases by defense attorneys. This system allows a defense attorney to compel a person to report to a location and answer unlimited questions that may fall far outside the subject matter. Most states prohibit this type of tactic; only Vermont, North Dakota, New Hampshire, and Florida consent to defense lawyers questioning victims outside a courtroom. Victims involved in sensitive crimes, such as rape, are subject to this discovery process. As expected, the defense contingent supports the concept and believes the system is aligned with justice. Prosecution groups and the American Bar Association have expressed their concern of the system as a method to intimidate witnesses.

CONCLUSION

Both prosecutors and defense attorneys have the ethical duty to uphold the laws of the State of Florida, but each attorney's responsibilities are to different individuals. The prosecutor's role in the criminal justice system is to ensure that society is afforded maximum execution of the laws enacted by the executive branch of government. Maximum execution means the reasonable pursuit of prosecution within the constraints and design of the criminal justice system. Some items that allow for prosecutorial discretion are the prosecutor's reasonable doubt that the accused is guilty, reluctance of the victim to testify, possible improper motives of a complainant, prolonged nonenforcement of a statute with community acquiescence, grand jury decisions regarding possible indictments, and the extent of harm caused by the offense. Defense attorneys are obligated to defend the accused to their fullest ability regardless of personal perceptions and convictions. All defendants have the right to be represented by an attorney, regardless of the financial status of the defendant. This right is guaranteed under the U.S. Constitution, under the 6th and 14th Amendments. This results in indigent individuals having public defenders appointed by the court having jurisdiction of the case against the defendant.

DISCUSSION QUESTIONS

1. Discuss the differences in the roles and responsibilities of the prosecution and the defense attorney.

2. Discuss the options a victim may have in filing a criminal complaint.

3. Discuss the function of a grand jury.

4. What is prosecutorial discretion?

5. Do criminals have a right to a defense attorney?

DEFINITIONS

Accessory—A person who aids, promotes, or contributes to the commission of a crime.

Acquittal—A judgment of a court, based on the verdict of a jury, that the defendant is not guilty of the offense.

Adjudicate—To judicially determine or decide.

Adversary system—A judicial system characterized by opposing parties.

Affidavit—A written statement sworn to or affirmed before an officer authorized to administer an oath or affirmation.

A.K.A.—Also known as.

Bail—To make bail means to obtain release from custody.

Case law—Law derived from reported court decisions.

Criminal contempt—A crime that consists of obstructing judicial duty, generally an act carried out in the presence of the court.

Defendant—The person accused of a crime in a criminal case.

Entrapment—Law enforcement agent inducing a person to commit a crime.

Grand jury—A jury consisting of 23 persons, selected according to law and sworn, whose duty it is to receive criminal complaints, hear the evidence put forth by the prosecution, and issue indictments when they are satisfied that there is probable cause that an accused person has committed a crime and should be brought to trial.

Habitual criminal—Person convicted of multiple offenses.

Incarceration—In jail or prison.

Indictment—A formal written accusation originating with a prosecutor and issued by a grand jury against a party charged with a crime. An indictment is referred to as a *true bill,* and failure to indict is called a *no bill.* An indictment is merely a charge that must be proved at trial beyond a reasonable doubt before a person can be convicted.

Indigent—A person indicted who is without funds or ability to hire a lawyer to defend him or her and who, on most instances, is entitled to appointed counsel, consistent with the protection of the 6th and 14th Amendments to the U.S. Constitution.

Liability—Legally obligated or responsible.

Mitigating circumstances—Circumstances that tend to minimize the offense or diminish responsibility.

Nolle prosequi—A formal entry on the record by the prosecuting officer by which he or she declares that he or she will not prosecute the case any further.

Nolo contendere—The defendant does not contest the charge. The plea is neither guilty or innocent.

Null—Void or invalid.

Petition—A written request made to the court.

Plea bargaining—Commonly, when the defendant pleads guilty to a lesser charge, may include a reduced sentence.

Prosecute—To initiate and maintain a criminal action against a person alleged to have committed an offense against the law in order to obtain a conviction.

Prosecuting witness—A private person whose complaint or information is the basis for a criminal accusation and who is the principal witness at the trial. Usually the prosecuting witness is the victim who is chiefly injured by the alleged crime.

Prosecutor—An attorney employed by a government agency whose official duty is to initiate and maintain criminal actions on behalf of the government against persons accused of committing crimes.

Prosecutorial screening decision—The decision of a prosecutor to submit a charging document to a court, to seek a grand jury indictment, or to decline to prosecute.

Quash—To make void.

Subpoena duces tecum—An order by the court to testify and bring evidence or required documents.

Verdict—A decision made by a judge or jury.

Voir dire—An examination of possible jurors or witnesses by the court or attorneys.

REFERENCES

Dade County State's Attorney Office, Miami, Fla.

CHAPTER 6

The Florida Courts

CHAPTER OVERVIEW

This chapter concentrates on the various judicial systems throughout the State of Florida, the purpose of each, and their interaction with one another and the community. A comprehensive examination of the process by which a defendant proceeds from being under investigation by the police to eventual acquittal or sentencing and appeal is provided. Additionally, the role and duties of the grand jury are explained as an integral component of the court system. The importance of the plea bargaining process to the prosecution, defense, and society is discussed, and its value to the entire court system is evaluated.

Traffic court, which is a section within the county court division, is examined, and an explanation of traffic infractions and traffic offenses, as well as the Affidavit of Defense, is provided.

Miami–Dade County Drug Court, a division of the circuit court, is an example of restructuring and innovation designed to relieve the overburdened court system. This court is examined to provide an understanding of the unique approaches of Florida's contemporary judicial system.

INTRODUCTION

More than 15,000 courts operate in the United States today (Harrigan, 1991). The United States operates under a dual court system, in which each state has its own court system in addition to a national court system (the federal courts).

The primary purpose of state and local courts is to resolve legal disputes. These disputes can be divided into two broad categories:

- *Tort:* Civil cases or "private" wrongs, such as breach of contract, personal injury, divorce, and probate. These cases arise when one individual or group sues another. The court will settle the dispute by either awarding damages or forcing one of the parties to act in a certain way (e.g., in a landlord–tenant matter, the court may force the tenant to move out of the rented property).

- *Crime:* "Public" wrongs, the criminal justice component of the courts. These cases arise when the government prosecutes an individual for violating the law. The court determines whether or not the accused is guilty and, if so, will also determine an appropriate sentence.

COURT ORGANIZATION

U.S. Supreme Court

The highest American court is the U.S. Supreme Court, which hears approximately 100 cases per year. Many of these cases have been heard in as many as three or four lower courts before making their way to the Supreme Court. The Supreme Court has jurisdiction over both federal and

The Federal Court System

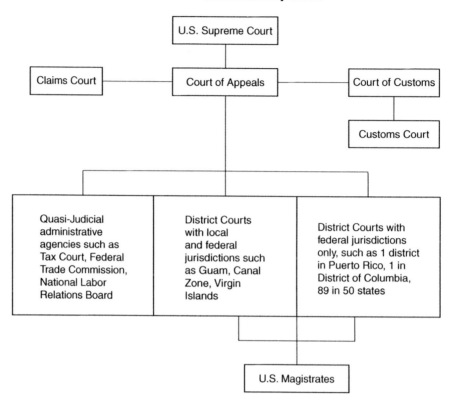

(*Source:* U.S. Courts, Washington, D.C., 2000.)

state systems. This is because the U.S. Constitution protects the rights of all criminal defendants (Cole and Smith, 1996).

State Courts

State courts are usually organized in a hierarchical structure. At the top is the state Supreme Court, which hears appeals from the state trial or lower appellate courts. Just below the supreme courts (in 37 states, including Florida) are appellate courts, which hear appeals from trial courts. At the bottom of the hierarchy are the trial courts.

Florida Court Organization

Prior to 1972, each municipality in Florida had the authority to have its own court system. In 1972, Florida citizens adopted Article V to the Florida Constitution that consolidated all Florida courts into a four-court system of two appellate and two trial courts. These are the district courts of appeals, circuit courts, and county courts. The Florida Constitution does not allow for any additional courts. Both circuit and county courts hear civil and criminal matters. Each county in Florida has its own court system comprised of circuit and county courts.

County courts have *original jurisdiction* over all misdemeanor (criminal) cases, all violations of municipal and county ordinances, and disputes in which the subject of controversy does not exceed $15,000. The county courts also hear all landlord–tenant disputes (regardless of the amount of money in question).

The circuit courts have original jurisdiction in all cases not vested in the county courts. These cases include criminal felonies, juveniles, and civil cases of over $15,000 (11th Judicial Circuit of Florida). It is at these (circuit and county) trial court levels that parties in the case present their testimony, facts are presented and examined, and a decision is made to resolve the dispute by the courts.

The Florida district courts of appeals hear appeals from the circuit and county courts. Courts of appeals do not decide cases based on facts (it is the responsibility of the trial courts to decide facts); rather, they decide whether the trial court applied the law properly.

The Florida Supreme Court is the highest court in Florida and consists of seven justices. Four justices must agree on a decision in each case. Justices are appointed by the Florida Governor and are retained by a "merit retention" vote every 4 years. The Florida Supreme Court must approve final orders imposing a death sentence and reviews district court decisions declaring state statutes or provisions of the state constitution invalid. In addition, the Supreme Court regulates the admission and discipline of lawyers in Florida (JOSHUA, 2003).

The Florida Court System

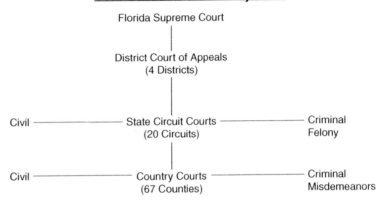

Florida Supreme Court

District Court of Appeals
(4 Districts)

Civil ———————— State Circuit Courts ———————— Criminal
(20 Circuits)   Felony

Civil ———————— Country Courts ———————— Criminal
(67 Counties)   Misdemeanors

Selection of Judges

Judges in Florida are selected in one of two ways. First, judges can either run for office or be appointed by the governor. Any member of the Florida bar who is a resident of the county in which he or she seeks office can run for election. These elections are nonpartisan and are held every 4 years for county court judges and every 6 years for circuit court judges. Second, in order to be appointed by the governor, a member of the Florida bar who is a resident in the county in which he or she seeks office must apply to the Judicial Nominating Committee, which consists of attorneys and laypeople. The committee selects three individuals and submits their names to the governor. The governor then appoints one of the three to be a judge. Once appointed, a judge must run for office within 1 year of his or her appointment (at the next general election) and again every 4 or 6 years, depending on whether he or she is a circuit or county court judge.

The Courts and Public Policy

Courts play an important role in establishing and implementing public policy and in resolving legal disputes. The courts do this by interpreting the law and, in the case of the Florida Supreme Court, determining whether a law is constitutional. This is called *judicial review*. When a law is declared unconstitutional by the Supreme Court, the law is no longer valid, and no one can be convicted for violating it (Harrigan, 1991).

THE JUSTICE PROCESS

Investigation

The criminal justice process begins when police believe a crime has been committed. Police depend largely on members of the community to report offenses. Once reported, an investigation into the crime is initiated.

Arrest

Once police determine that a crime has been committed and that a particular person likely committed it, they place the suspect under arrest and, in most cases, take the suspect to county jail. In some cases, arrests are made based on a *warrant*. In this case, a court order is issued by a judge authorizing police to make an arrest. Most cases, however, are made without a warrant.

Booking

After the arrested individual has been brought to jail, a series of administrative steps takes place in a process known as *booking*. This involves entry of the person's name, the crime for which the arrest was made, and other relevant facts into the police blotter. In addition, the individual's photographs and fingerprints are taken, and a description of the individual's physical appearance is noted. Booking may also include an interrogation by police and identification of the suspect in a police lineup.

Charging

After the accused is booked, all information relevant to the case is turned over to the prosecutor. The prosecutor will then evaluate the facts and determine whether there is reasonable cause to believe the crime was committed by the suspect. The decision to charge is solely the prosecutor's. The prosecutor can decide not to charge the individual, in which case the suspect is released.

Initial Appearance

After the suspect has been booked, he or she must appear before a judge, usually within 48 hours. The judge will state the charges against the suspect, advise the suspect of his or her rights, and set bail. (Sometimes the offense does not warrant bail). The judge then decides if there is sufficient evidence to hold the suspect for additional criminal processing (Cole and Smith, 1996). If the judge decides evidence is insufficient to justify holding the defendant further, the judge will dismiss the case. During the initial appearance stage, a defendant is entitled to an attorney. If the defendant is indigent, counsel will be appointed to represent him or her.

Bail

As stated earlier, bail is usually set during the initial appearance. Bail involves the accused depositing money (or in some cases other valuables) in exchange for release from custody until trial. This practice is called *pre-trial release*. In some cases, an alternative to cash bail is available. Such alternatives include release on recognizance (where the defendant guarantees in writing that he or she will return for trial), conditional release (where the defendant must attend programs such as a drug treatment course), and property bond (where the defendant must use property or other valuables as collateral for his or her release). The purpose of bail is to ensure that defendants will appear for trial. Bail also prevents people who have not been convicted of a crime from being unnecessarily imprisoned (Schmallenger, 1991). Bail is usually set in accordance with the seriousness of the crime and the defendants' prior criminal record. If the defendant has a lengthy criminal record and the crime is serious, it is likely that the amount of bail set by the judge will be high. If the offense is not serious, it is possible for the defendant to be released on his or her own recognizance (that is, a promise made by the defendant to return for trial). A defendant who cannot afford bail can borrow the appropriate amount from a bail-bondsperson, who will loan the defendant the money at a high interest rate (usually 10%) which must be paid before release.

Most defendants have the opportunity to be released prior to their trial. Approximately 85% of state-level defendants and 82% of federal defendants are afforded this opportunity (Schmallenger, 1991).

Preliminary Hearing/Grand Jury

This stage involves the defendant appearing before a judge, who will again summarize the charges, and the defendant will be advised of his or her rights. This hearing is similar to a trial in that the prosecution often presents witnesses and evidence in support of the prosecution's complaint. The defendant also has the right to testify and present witnesses and evidence. The preliminary hearing gives the defendant the opportunity to challenge the legal basis for his or her detention. The purpose of this hearing is for the judge to decide if there is probable cause that a crime has been committed and that the defendant committed the crime. It is not necessary for the defendant's guilt to be decided beyond a reasonable doubt, only that there is sufficient evidence that the defendant committed the crime. If the judge is satisfied that there is sufficient evidence to justify a trial, then the case proceeds directly to the grand jury (only required in capital cases in Florida) or to trial.

Grand Jury

The function of the grand jury in criminal matters is to investigate and determine whether there is sufficient evidence to justify an indictment against an accused. The grand jury must decide whether there is probable cause that a crime has been committed by the person accused. If they determine that the evidence is sufficient to constitute probable cause, they issue a *true bill,* which then becomes the indictment on which the accused will be tried. State's attorneys must attend hearings of the grand jury for the purpose of examining witnesses in their presence, giving legal advice in any matter before them, and preparing bills of indictment. Prosecutors are not required to obtain grand jury indictments, except in capital crimes, in order to bring someone to trial. The Florida Constitution guarantees that "no person shall be tried for a capital crime without presentment or indictment by a grand jury" (Article I, Section 15a). Capital crimes are felonies for which the penalty is life imprisonment or death.

The grand jury consists of 23 men and women selected at random who decide whether or not there is sufficient evidence to justify an *indictment* against a defendant. An indictment is a formal accusation by the grand jury or the prosecution. Again, in Florida, it is not necessary to have an indictment from the grand jury unless the crime is a **capital crime.**

Grand jury hearings are not held in public, and the defendant may not attend them. The grand jury hears evidence from the prosecution only and has the authority to subpoena witnesses and records. When the grand jury determines there is sufficient evidence that a crime occurred and that the suspect committed it, it issues a true bill or an indictment charging the individual with the crime. If it finds that there is insufficient evidence that the suspect committed the crime, it issues a *no bill* and the case is dismissed.

Indictment/Information

If the grand jury issues a true bill or if the judge in the preliminary hearing decides there is sufficient evidence to charge the defendant, then the prosecution enters a formal indictment, or *information,* before the court.

Arraignment

Once a defendant has been formally indicted by a grand jury or an information has been filed by the prosecution, the defendant is formally charged with the crime. The defendant appears before a judge, who will state the charges, and the defendant enters a plea. It is important to note that often the crime for which the defendant was originally arrested is not necessarily the crime for which the defendant will be tried. In the course of investigations that take place after arrests, evidence may indicate that additional crimes were committed or that a different crime was committed. The defendant can enter one of three pleas: (1) guilty, (2) not guilty, or (3) *nolo contendere* (no contest). The defendant can refuse to enter a plea, in which case a plea of not guilty will be entered by the court. If the defendant pleads guilty, the judge must be sure that the defendant has full knowledge of the possible consequences of such a plea and that the defendant entered the guilty plea voluntarily. If the defendant pleads guilty, no trial and sentencing follow. It is at this stage that plea bargaining usually takes place (although a plea bargain can be reached at any time throughout the criminal justice process). Few criminal cases actually go to trial, as most cases move directly from a guilty plea to the sentencing stage (Cole and Smith, 1996).

Plea Bargaining

Plea bargaining occurs when the prosecution and the defense agree to the defendant entering a guilty plea in exchange for a determined sentence. Plea bargaining is advantageous to the prosecution because it results in a quick conviction rather than a lengthy trial. In addition, in cases where the prosecution's case is weak, plea bargaining provides assurance of a conviction. Plea bargaining is advantageous to the defendant because it often guarantees a reduced sentence because of the defendant's cooperation. Defense attorneys may be eager for their clients to accept a plea bargain when they are unsure of their ability to win acquittal at trial.

Plea bargaining is a common practice in American courts today. In some jurisdictions, as many as 90% of all criminal cases are resolved through a plea bargain (Schmallenger, 1991). Plea bargaining dramatically decreases the number of cases that proceed through courts in the United States. Without plea bargaining, our criminal justice system would likely come to a halt, as it is simply not designed to handle the vast amount of cases that move through prosecutors' offices. In addition, plea bargaining leads to a prompt and final disposition of most criminal cases (Cole and Smith, 1996).

Critics of plea bargaining claim that it allows offenders to escape the severe punishments they deserve. Attorneys and judges respond to this criticism by claiming that plea bargaining benefits society by allowing decision makers within the criminal justice system to attain *individualized* justice (Cole and Smith, 1996).

Trial

The Sixth Amendment to the U.S. Constitution guarantees the right to a trial by an impartial jury to every defendant who faces charges serious enough to result in possible imprisonment for more than 6 months (Cole and Smith, 1996). It is during the trial phase of the criminal justice process that evidence is presented to the judge or jury and that the guilt or innocence of the accused is decided. Trials are held in about 9% of all criminal felony cases in the United States. Of these, 5% are jury trials and 4% are bench trials (Cole and Smith, 1996).

Jury Trials

Jury trials are utilized in both criminal or civil cases. Trial juries traditionally consist of 12 men and women selected at random from the community in which the trial takes place.

In Florida, criminal jury trials are held before a jury of 6 men and women (or 12 in capital cases) who decide whether or not the accused is guilty. In death penalty cases, the jury also makes recommendations as to whether or not the defendant should be sentenced to death. In civil cases, the jury decides who should be awarded monetary damages and oftentimes the amounts (Harrigan, 1991).

A defendant is entitled to a jury trial under the following circumstances:

- The prosecution is seeking to incarcerate the defendant.

- The prosecution is seeking to adjudicate the defendant.

- The offense carries a maximum sentence of more than one year (even if the prosecution is not seeking a maximum sentence)

- The statute requires it (as in the case of the Florida DUI law, where a jury trial is allowed in the statute).

In order for a criminal defendant to be declared guilty, the jury must unanimously decide the defendant's guilt "beyond and to the exclusion of a reasonable doubt" (Harrigan, 1991). It is often difficult to reach such unanimity with 12 people. Because of this, many states have reduced the 12-member jury requirement to 6 (as in Florida). Other states have changed the law to require a majority vote instead of a unanimous vote.

Bench Trials

Bench trials are held before a judge without a jury. The judge is solely responsible for declaring the accused guilty or not guilty. Bench trials are held when the offense carries a maximum sentence of less than one year, when the prosecution is not seeking to adjudicate or incarcerate the defendant, or when defendants waive their right to a jury trial.

Role of the Judge in Criminal Trials

The judge's primary responsibility during a criminal trial is to ensure justice. The judge must safeguard the rights of the defendant and the interests of the public. The judge decides matters of law, decides the admissibility of evidence, and weighs objections in the courtroom. In instances where the defendant has waived the right to a jury or is not entitled to a jury trial, the judge decides the guilt or innocence of the defendant. The judge, in most jurisdictions, also sentences offenders once they have been found guilty (Schmallenger, 1991).

Judges serve many functions while on the bench. First and foremost, they are adjudicators. They are the neutral decisionmakers who issue rulings based on arguments and evidence presented by the defense and prosecution. Judges make these rulings in accordance with the law. The law, however, allows for discretion on the part of the judge in making decisions. For example, sentences usually must be imposed in accordance with sentencing guidelines established by the Florida legislature. A significant difference often exists between the minimum and maximum sentences for a specific violation. The judge must impose a sentence within those guidelines, but it is up to the judge to decide whether to impose the maximum sentence, the minimum sentence, or a sentence somewhere in between the two (Cole and Smith, 1996).

Judges also spend much of their time in chambers with prosecutors and defense attorneys attempting to facilitate communication and compromise between the attorneys. In less serious cases, the judge may do this from the bench. This allows for an easier resolution of many cases in the pretrial phases of the criminal justice process (Cole and Smith, 1996).

THE TRIAL PROCESS

Jury Selection

The first stage of the trial process is jury selection. Jury selection technically takes place before the trial formally begins. This stage is important because it establishes the decisionmakers in the case. Each month, jury pools are drawn from which a jury will be selected by the prosecution and the defense for trials. Attorneys seek to identify potential jurors who will be sympathetic or hostile to their side and will either select them for the jury or eliminate them.

In the jury selection process, attorneys for both sides and the judge question potential jurors to eliminate people who may be biased or incapable of rendering a fair verdict. This process is called *voir dire* ("to speak the truth"). The attorneys and the judge will question the potential jurors about their background, knowledge of the case, and knowledge of any of the participants in the case. If, in the course of questioning these potential jurors, either of the attorneys feels a juror will not be able to make a fair decision, the juror may be *challenged for cause* and excused from the jury (the judge must rule on this challenge). There is no limit to the number of jurors that the attorneys can challenge for cause (Cole and Smith, 1996).

Attorneys can also dismiss potential jurors from the jury using *peremptory challenges*. These challenges can be used to exclude jurors without the necessity of providing specific reasons to the judge. The prosecution is usually allowed six to eight peremptory challenges, and the defense eight to ten. These challenges are normally used to dismiss jurors who the attorneys feel will be unsympathetic to their position.

Opening Statements

Once the jury has been selected, the trial begins with the clerk of the court reading the indictment or information containing the charges against the defendant. The attorneys then make an opening statement to the jury. Each side attempts to provide a preview of what they expect to prove during the trial. Opening statements are not considered evidence; therefore, the jury will be instructed not to consider opening statements as proof during deliberations.

Presentation of Evidence

A defendant is presumed innocent until proven guilty. Because of this, it is the prosecution that bears the burden of proving the guilt of the defendant beyond a reasonable doubt. The prosecution begins by presenting its evidence to the jury, and once the prosecution has concluded the defense presents its evidence.

Several strategies are available to the defense attorney. The defense may attempt to disprove or cast doubt on the prosecution's evidence by presenting its own testimony or experts. In addition, the defense attorney can try to offer an alibi by proving that the defendant could not have committed the crime. The defense may also present evidence that the defendant was either acting in self defense or was mentally insane.

One of the more difficult decisions the defense has to make is whether or not to have the defendant testify on his or her own behalf. The Fifth Amendment protects criminal defendants from being compelled to testify against themselves, and the jury is not permitted to infer guilt from a defendant not testifying. Defendants who agree to testify are left vulnerable to cross-examination from the prosecution. This creates opportunities for the prosecution to elicit information from a defendant that may otherwise not be obtained from evidence, such as a defendant's past criminal record. Many defense attorneys choose not to have their clients testify because the risks are too great (Cole and Smith, 1996).

There are four basic types of evidence

1. *Real evidence* includes physical objects, such as weapons, stolen property, forensic samples, documents, records, or other objects found at the scene of the crime. Testimony, or oral evidence, is the most common type of evidence in a criminal trial.

2. *Testimony* is a statement made in court by people related to the case, such as police officers.

3. *Direct evidence* is an eyewitness account from someone who witnessed the crime.

4. *Circumstantial evidence* requires that the judge or jury infer a fact from information that has been presented. For example, if an eyewitness states that he saw the defendant running from the scene of the crime, the prosecution will want the jury to infer that the defendant was running to flee from police.

Rebuttal Witnesses

Once the defense has concluded its case, the prosecution has the opportunity to present witnesses who will attempt to discredit the defense witnesses. These rebuttal witnesses will then be cross-examined by the defense.

Closing Arguments

Closing arguments are the final phase of the trial. This is an opportunity for the attorneys on each side to appeal directly to the jury. Closing arguments from the prosecution usually summarize the case and correlate the evidence to the elements of the crime. Closing arguments from the defense usually emphasize weaknesses in the prosecution's case.

Jury Instructions

Once each side has presented its case and closing arguments have concluded, the judge will give guidelines to the jury that will set the framework for the jury's deliberation and verdict. These instructions explain to the jury how to properly evaluate evidence presented during the trial. The judge determines the law that applies to the case; therefore, the judge's instructions are critical to the outcome of the case. In fact, many appeals are won because of improper jury instructions.

The jury is instructed that, in order to find the defendant guilty, the jurors must believe unanimously that the prosecution has proven its case *beyond a reasonable doubt,* which means that "a juror is satisfied to a moral certainty that the defendant . . . is guilty of the crime(s) charged." Once the jury retires to the jury room, they elect a foreperson who will guide deliberations and announce the verdict.

Sentencing

If the jury finds the defendant guilty, it is the judge's responsibility to sentence the defendant. Sentencing usually occurs after the trial, and the defendant is customarily detained in the local county jail until that time. In Florida, the prosecution commonly advises the judge of the sentencing guidelines (set by the legislature) for the offense. If the judge desires to punish the defendant more or less severely than the sentencing guidelines allow, the judge must publicly (in the court record) state why.

Appeals

An appellate court does not reconsider facts in a case; rather, it considers the basis of law that was used in the lower court. The appeals process provides a means of ensuring the accuracy of legal decisions affecting a defendant. Appellate decisions also affect the way the law is interpreted by different judges. For example, if judges are interpreting a specific section of criminal code differently, the appellate decision will clarify the issue for all judges. Defendants who win on appeal do not usually go free; rather, they are usually retried without the contested evidence or with different jury instructions.

DRUG COURT, MIAMI–DADE COUNTY, FLORIDA

Miami–Dade County Circuit Court has a unique pilot program designed as a means of alleviating prison overcrowding that has been studied by cities throughout the country as an alternate means of relieving an overburdened criminal justice system. The concept behind the Miami–Dade County, Florida Drug Court, which commenced in May of 1989, has greatly changed over the years as defendants began using the Drug Court as a means of avoiding lengthy prison sentences. The program was designed to be a program to divert first-time drug offenders from court calendars and to keep them from being incarcerated by emphasizing treatment over punishment and rehabilitation over jail. Defendants in this program are subject to a variety of treatments and monitoring, including acupuncture, counseling, and court-monitored urine tests. If the defendant remains drug free for a sufficient amount of time in accordance with the court, the criminal charges may be dropped, and the court upon request seals the records of the defendant. Sealing a record is different from purging a record. To purge is the total removal of criminal information. Sealing is done by the court and prevents general access to criminal information. The period of time for which a defendant can remain in the program depends upon the defendant's behavior, progress, and commitment to the program. Typically, the time defendants spend in the program ranges from 4 months to 4 years.

After 10 years in existence, the success of the Drug Court is debatable. It remains a model program throughout the country, although the recidivism rate of participants has not been fully evaluated and measured. Of over 7000 participants, varying evaluation methods have produced diverse results; successful graduation from the program has ranged from 20% to slightly higher than 65%. Also, approximately 2000 participants have had warrants issued for their arrest since the program began because of their failure to conclude the program as ordered. The scope of the program has expanded several times in the last few years and now includes repeat offenders and dangerous criminals, as well as the initial first-time drug offender.

FLORIDA TRAFFIC COURT

Introduction

Prior to 1972, Florida's court system contained 14 different styles of courts. Almost every community created its own independent court, many of whom produced their own territorial fees and standards for justice. A revision to the judicial article of the state constitution on March 14, 1972, eliminated the divergent combination of courts throughout the state. A new system emerged consolidating two levels of appellate court and two levels of trial court. By 1975, all municipal and local courts were abolished and the controversial traffic court was absorbed into the county-level court component.

Florida Uniform Traffic Control Law

The legislature passed the Uniform Traffic Control Law to unify and standardize traffic laws throughout the state, including all communities and municipalities. It is unlawful for any local authority to pass or attempt to enforce an ordinance in conflict with provisions of the motor vehicle chapter.

Traffic Violations

The Florida rules of traffic court divide traffic violations into two categories: traffic infraction and traffic offense. A *traffic infraction* is a noncriminal traffic violation that is not punishable by incarceration and for which there is no right to a jury or a court-appointed attorney. A *traffic offense* is a violation that may subject a defendant upon conviction to incarceration within the county.

EXAMPLES OF TRAFFIC INFRACTIONS

316.614: Safety belt usage
316.183: Unlawful speed
316.610: Vehicle inspection

EXAMPLES OF TRAFFIC OFFENSES

316.192: Reckless driving
316.193: Driving under the influence
322.34: Driving while license suspended

Traffic Infraction

A traffic infraction may be addressed by mail under certain circumstances. A written statement of facts along with an affidavit of defense (see Figure 1) should be submitted to the court within 30 days of the infraction date. Penalties for civil infractions may not exceed $500.00. Additionally, any points accumulated on a driving record for a non-criminal traffic infraction are expunged after 3 years from posting.

Figure 1

Affidavit of Defense

_____
(Name of Alleged Offender)

_____
(Number of Complaint)

IN THE COUNTY COURT,

IN AND FOR _____ COUNTY, FLORIDA

Before me, personally appeared _____
                                      (Name of Alleged Offender)

who having been duly sworn, deposes and says:

My name is _____; I reside permanently at _____

_____, and I received the above numbered
                (Street and No.)

complaint charging me with _____
                                      (Description of Violation)

on _____ at _____AM-PM.
      (Date)   (Time)

At the time of the alleged violation, I was driving a _____
                                                        (Type of Motor Vehicle)

in a _____ on _____in
        (Direction)   (Street or Avenue)

_____County, Florida.

I am leaving _____ County on _____ and my hearing date is
                                              (Date)

_____ at Court Location _____at
      (Date)   (Location)

_____.
      (Time)

I am DENYING/ADMITTING (strike one) the commission of the infraction because: (Explain your defense in your own words, being as brief as possible, but omitting no material facts that will help the official arrive at a judgment in your case.)

(IF MORE SPACE IS NEEDED FOR EXPLANATION - USE REVERSE SIDE.)

_____
Signature of Affiant (Defendant)

Sworn to and subscribed before me, this _____ day of _____, 20_____.

_____
Signature of Deputy Clerk, County Court

or Notary Public

NOTE: This affidavit will be represented to the presiding official together with the complaint against you, on the date noted on your copy of the complaint or as soon thereafter as possible. You will be advised by mail of the result, and will, at that time, receive from the court a check covering the balance of your bond, after deduction of penalty, if any is imposed. The judges of this court reserve the right to compel personal appearance as may be determined by the gravity or seriousness of the offense charged.

(_Source_: FDLE. 1998.)

Traffic Offense Procedure

A traffic offense is a misdemeanor that normally requires a court appearance. Because some violations may prescribe time in the county jail, a court-appointed attorney may be available. In traffic offense cases, the State of Florida files charges alleging a criminal violation; under the constitution, the defendant has the right to plead not guilty, demand a trail by jury, refuse to testify, and compel witnesses to attend the trial. Because traffic offenses are misdemeanors, the State must prove its case beyond and to the exclusion of every reasonable doubt. The formal procedural steps are as follows:

1. *Arraignment:* The driving offense is explained, including the penalties and defendant's rights. A plea is entered.

2. *Trial:* Approximately 3 to 4 weeks after arraignment, the State will present evidence and call witnesses to support its case. The defendant has the right to question the witnesses. The defendant presents the evidence and calls witnesses. The prosecution has the right to question witnesses. Both the prosecution and the defense present final statements.

3. *Burden of proof:* The plea of not guilty requires the court to presume the defendant is innocent; therefore, the State must prove that a crime was committed and that the defendant committed the offense.

4. *Reasonable doubt:* A reasonable doubt is not a possible doubt or imaginary or forced doubt. If after carefully considering, comparing, and weighing all the evidence, there is not an abiding conviction of guilt or if, having a conviction, it is one which is not stable but one which wavers and vacillates, then the charge is not proven beyond reasonable doubt.

5. *Verdict:* Only one verdict may be returned as to the traffic offense charged.

   • *Not guilty:* Based upon the verdict, the court or jury finding the defendant not guilty of the offense charged in the charging document in criminal number ___, the court now adjudges the defendant not guilty of the traffic offense, and the matter is discharged.

   • *Guilty:* Having been found guilty by the court or jury of the charge of ___ as contained in case number ___, the court now finds the defendant guilty of the traffic offense ___ and adjudge the defendant guilty.

6. *Sentencing:* The punishment is assigned to the defendant.

Traffic Ticket Recipients

South Florida has a disproportionately high elderly population; however, residents who are 65 or older receive fewer traffic tickets than the general population. Males comprise approximately 59% of the population in Miami–Dade County; however, they receive about 76% of all traffic tickets. Younger drivers appear more likely to receive a traffic violation: In Miami–Dade County, drivers who are less than 20 years of age account for about 2.3% of the drivers; however, they receive about 7% of the citations.

Statistics published by the Federal government, indicate that nationally recorded traffic violations of the 55 mph speed limit decreased about 6.5%, 7.5 million to 7 million from 1988 to 1992. In the State of Florida, the number of traffic citations overall decreased about 11% from 1989 to 1993. Due to public concern about crime, the focus of law enforcement may be applying different approaches to police patrol.

The Code of Judicial Conduct

Judges are an important part of the criminal justice system, as they interpret and apply laws within the justice system. A judge is an arbitrator of facts of law for the resolution of disputes, conflicts, and accusations. Conduct of personnel in the judiciary branch is an important aspect of perceiving fairness in the courts. The Code of Judicial Conduct establishes standards for ethical conduct of judges. It consists of broad statements called *cannons,* which are specific rules that include definitions and guidance for the judiciary. The following are the seven basic cannons for judicial conduct:

1. A judge shall uphold the integrity and independence of the judiciary.

2. A judge shall avoid impropriety and the appearance of impropriety in all of the judge's activities.

3. A judge shall perform the duties of judicial office impartially and diligently.

4. A judge may engage in activities to improve the law, the legal system, and the administration of justice.

5. A judge shall regulate extrajudicial activities to minimize the risk of conflict with judicial duties:

    a. Extrajudicial activities in general

    b. Avocational activities

    c. Governmental, civic, or charitable activities

    d. Financial activities

    e. Fiduciary activities

    f. Service as arbitrator or mediator

    g. Practice of law

6. Fiscal matters of a judge shall be conducted in a manner that does not give the appearance of influence or impropriety; a judge shall regularly file public reports as required by Article II, Section 8, of the Constitution of Florida, and shall publicly report gifts; additional financial information shall be filed with the judicial qualifications commission to ensure full financial disclosure:

    a. Compensation for quasi-judicial and extrajudicial services and reimbursement of expenses

    b. Public financial reporting

    c. Confidential financial reporting to the judicial qualifications commission

    d. Limitation of disclosure

7. A judge or candidate for judicial office shall refrain from inappropriate politial activity:

    a. All judges and candidates

    b. Candidates seeking appointment to judicial or other governmental office

    c. Judges and candidates subject to public election

    d. Incumbent judges

    e. Applicability

CONCLUSION

Courts, ranging from the U.S. Supreme Court to county courts, have a common, primary purpose—to resolve legal disputes. The hierarchical structure of Florida's judicial system incorporates checks and balances to ensure justice for all citizens involved in the process. Each court within the State of Florida is designed for a specific purpose. The Florida's Supreme Court reviews district court decisions declaring state statutes or provisions of the state constitution invalid, as well as approving final orders imposing death sentences and regulating the admission and discipline of Florida's attorneys. The four district courts of appeals hear appeals from the circuit and county courts, but only decide whether the trial court applied the law properly. They do not decide cases based upon the facts. The 20 circuit courts have jurisdiction in all cases not vested in the county courts, and they hear criminal felony, juvenile, and civil cases in amounts over $15,000 in controversy. Florida's 67 county courts have original jurisdiction over all misdemeanor criminal cases, all violations of municipal and county ordinances, and disputes that do not exceed $15,000 in controversy.

The process through which a defendant moves through the criminal justice system in a criminal matter can be very involved, starting with a police investigation leading to an arrest, booking, charging, initial appearance, bail, preliminary hearing/grand jury, indictment/information, arraignment, plea bargaining, trial (jury or bench), sentencing, and appeal. The defendant is entitled to counsel under the Sixth Amendment of the United States. If the defendant is determined to be indigent, a court-appointed attorney is assigned. Finally, a few selected definitions are provided to enhance an understanding of the judicial system.

DISCUSSION QUESTIONS

1. Identify the steps in the justice process.

2. What is the function of the Florida grand jury?

3. What is plea bargaining?

4. Discuss the different stages of a trial.

5. What is the difference between a traffic infraction and a traffic offense?

DEFINITIONS

Adjudicate—Judicially determine or decide.

Appeal—An application to or proceeding in an appellate court for review or rehearing of a judgment, decision, or order of a lower court in order to correct alleged errors or injustices in the trial below.

Appellate Court—A court that hears appeals of decisions of lower courts but does not try cases.

Arrest—The taking of a person into the custody of the law for purpose of charging the person with a criminal offense.

Bail—To obtain release from custody.

Bench trial—A nonjury trial.

Booking—A police administrative procedure officially recording an arrest in a police register.

Capital crime—A crime which is punishable by death or imprisonment for life.

Challenged for cause—A formal objection to a prospective juror.

Charge—To formally accuse a specified person of committing a specific crime.

Circumstantial evidence—Requires the judge or jury to infer a fact from information that has been presented.

Crimes—A "public" wrong or any act done in violation of the law.

Controversy—An actual dispute between persons who seek judicial resolution of grievances arising from a conflict of their alleged legal rights.

Direct evidence—An eyewitness account from someone who witnessed the crime.

Dual court system—Judicial structure consisting of one national court system and a state court system for each individual state.

Indictment—A formal, written, accusation from the grand jury, alleging that a specific person or persons committed a crime or crimes.

Infraction—A violation of state statute or local ordinance punishable by fine or other penalty, but not by incarceration.

Judicial review—The power of the courts to review decisions of another department or level of government.

Jurisdiction—The legal and geographical range of a court's authority.

Jury—A body of persons, selected and sworn according to law, to inquire into certain matters of fact and to render a verdict based on evidence presented before them.

Jury trial—A trial in which a jury determines the issues of fact and renders a guilty or not guilty verdict.

Original jurisdiction—The court's authority to hear the original case.

Offense—An act committed or omitted in violation of a law forbidding or commanding it.

Plea bargaining—The exchange of prosecutorial or judicial concessions, or both, in return for a guilty plea.

Peremptory challenge—A formal objection to a prospective juror for which no reason needs to be given.

Quasi-judicial—Like or almost judicial.

Quash—To annul or make void.

Quid Pro Quo—"Something for something;" one thing in exchange for another (e.g., the reduction in charge was the *quid pro quo* for the defendant's plea of guilty).

Real evidence—Includes physical objects, such as weapons, stolen property, forensic samples, documents, records, or other objects found at the scene of a crime.

Reasonable doubt—The standard used to determine the guilt or innocence of a person charged with a crime.

Record—An officially written statement of an act or transaction designed to be preserved as evidence of the act or transaction.

Release on bail—A pretrial release in which reappearance is guaranteed by a pledge that money or property will be forfeited upon nonappearance.

Seal—Sealing a record is different from purging a record. Purging is total removal of criminal information; sealing is done by the court and prevents general access to criminal information.

Supreme court—The highest appellate court in the United States federal court system and in the court systems of most states.

Testimony—Statement made in court by people related to the case.

Torts—A "private" or civil wrong or injury.

Traffic offenses—A group of offenses including infractions and very minor misdemeanors relating to the operation of self-propelled motor vehicles.

Trial—The examination in court of issues of fact and law in a case for the purpose of reaching a judgment.

Voir Dire—An examination by the court or attorneys of prospective jurors or witnesses to determine if they are competent or qualified for service.

Warrant—A written order issued by a judicial officer or other authorized person commanding a law enforcement officer to perform some act incident to the administration of justice.

REFERENCES

Cole, G. F. and C. E. Smith. 1996. *Criminal Justice in America.* Belmont, Calif.: Wadsworth Publishing.

Eleventh Judicial Circuit of Florida, Administrative Office of the Court, *Progress Report 1990–1995.*

(FDLE). 1998. *The Law Enforcement Handbook.* Tallahassee, Fla.: Florida Department of Law Enforcement.

Harrigan, J. J. 1991. *Politics and Policy in States and Communities.* New York: HarperCollins.

JOSHUA. 2003. http://justice.courts.state.fl.us/courts/supct/system/html.

Schmallenger, F. 1991. *Criminal Justice Today.* Englewood Cliffs, N.J.: Prentice Hall.

CHAPTER **7**

College Education, Internships, Selection Process, and Ancillary Professions

CHAPTER OVERVIEW

This chapter concentrates on the various employment avenues available within the criminal justice field on local, county, state, and federal levels. Public police fields, ancillary professions, and privatized services are discussed, and specific means of contacting those agencies are provided. The educational level of the criminal justice professional is changing, so the benefits of obtaining college-level education are analyzed. Also provided in this chapter is a discussion of internships and the national criminal justice college honor society which may offer alternative opportunities to those interested in entering criminal justice as a profession. Finally, the chapter reviews the application and selection process involved in gaining employment with a criminal justice agency.

COLLEGE EDUCATION IN CRIMINAL JUSTICE

Challenges for Law Enforcement in Florida

The complex contemporary society of Florida creates a variety of new and unique problems for police. The State of Florida has a population of rich diversity that is now in excess of 13,000,000 people. The challenges Florida law enforcement officers will face in the future require an educated approach to law enforcement. New concepts in the delivery of police service have emerged as viable alternatives to traditional styles.

Complexity of Modern Problems

The concept of *community policing* is an approach to urban problems that requires police officers to be problem solvers and advisors to the community. Moreover, the police officer deploys strategies contingent upon analysis of the problem. The role of a police officer shifts from a reactive approach to systematic and objective analysis of problems that may require a college-level education. Additionally, several new models for police investigation, crime detection, crime control, and police management demand advanced educational skills. Advocates of higher education for police point out that the modern police officer must have the ability to analyze and understand complex materials and investigations, write clear and comprehensive reports documenting at times very complicated criminal events, and react appropriately to people of different cultures and people with varied problems and perceptions. The complexity of the population of Florida requires police to be pragmatic, with the objective of reducing or eliminating a problem, not just reacting to disorder in the community. This analytical approach to policing requires the police officer to understand an array of concepts, including the functions of social services, city and county operations, and state and federal structures. Additionally, it appears that a correlation exists between college-educated police officers and police civil-liability issues. Many police and city officials suggest police abuses are less likely when officers are college educated.

Educational Recommendations

Several national police leaders have recommended that education may be one of the solutions to the problem of the intricate job of policing South Florida. The list of proponents of college education for police both nationally and locally are extensive. The President's Commission of Law Enforcement and Administration of Justice, the National Advisory Commission on Civil Disorders, the National Commission on the Causes and Prevention of Violence, the American Bar Association Project on Criminal Justice, the National Advisory Commission on Criminal Justice Standards and Goals, and the National Advisory Commission on Higher Education for Police Officers all support the concept that college education is an excellent vehicle for improving and reforming criminal justice.

Davis v. Dallas

In *Davis v. City of Dallas,* 777 F. 2nd 205 (5th Circuit Court of Appeals), the court held that a 45-semester-hour college requirement for entry employment was sufficiently job related to offset any discriminatory effects. The most important issue in the case was that college education is a *bona fide* occupational qualification for a police officer. There appears to be a high level of interest among Florida police agencies, both at the federal and local levels, for requiring college education.

Benefits of College Education for Police

The by-products of police college education are numerous; many studies indicate that performance improves with college. A study reported by Kappeler et al. (1990) found that police officers who had a 4-year college degree were targets of significantly fewer founded public complaints than other police officers. Other studies report that college-educated police officers evaluate and select better solutions to problems than non-college-educated police officers, which is particularly important for the new philosophy of community policing wherein police are given a higher degree of freedom to select appropriate solutions when dealing with people.

The Florida Department of Law Enforcement (1993) indicates that police and correctional officers total more than 68,000. Only about 30% have education beyond high school. Moreover, 81% of officers accused of serious immoral or criminal conduct who were required to appear before the state commission had limited education, high school level or less. The records of the Criminal Justice Standards and Training Commission indicate that over 75% of all disciplinary action cases occur among officers with education confined to high school. In 1993, officers with college degrees represented 19% of the 68,000; however, college-educated officers represented only 10% of all officers called before the board that issues state commissions for officers.

Law Enforcement as a Profession

Law enforcement agency accreditation has moved the position of police officer closer to professional status. Many police agencies have undergone extensive adjustment and scrutiny to accomplish that standing; however, total professional status requires formal training with an intellectual component, certification of competence, demonstrated ability, mechanisms to ensure responsible behavior, and a commitment to research and enhancement of knowledge. Training provides the police officer with technical competence, and a university education provides intellectual exploration, research, and discussion.

Transformation of aggregate education levels in an occupation can lead to a transformation of the nature of the job. Historically, law and medicine have been transformed and improved as a direct result of increased educational requirements (Sherman, 1978).

The Criminal Justice Internship

In terms of discipline, criminal justice explores interdisciplinary scholarly teaching and research in the behavioral and social sciences focusing on the social problem of crime (Myren, 1982). Internships in the field of criminal justice may be one of the most important encounters of pre-employment. This experience provides an opportunity to develop relationships with practitioners, as well as first-hand engagement with components of the criminal justice system. Internships were developed in the Middle Ages as a method of passing on skills and competencies in trades. This concept continues in many professions today, such as law, medicine, counseling, and education. Internships within the field of criminal justice provide an opportunity to learn how a particular agency or division functions.

What Is a Criminal Justice Internship?

Internships were designed to allow students the opportunity to apply academic training to practical experience. The career-related experience will permit students to bridge the theories and knowledge learned in the classroom with the working complexities of the criminal justice system. This experience may assist the student in recognizing the numerous options available in the profession and provide the opportunity to network in the field. The field encounter exposes the interns to essential information that may help clarify their career decisions; work in the field allows students to make critical adjustments in their career paths, thus possibly impacting agency retention.

The Florida Department of Corrections provides students with an opportunity to learn marketable skills and affords part-time compensation in its formal internship program. The program enhances staff productivity while allowing for students' professional networking. This opportunity is available at most correction facilities throughout the State of Florida.

Selection and Placement

Most internship programs are processed through educational institutions as a college-level course with degree-earning credits; however, it is possible to obtain internship placement outside of the college environment. In either approach, the process involves:

- selecting a component of criminal justice of interest (courts/police/corrections)
- researching local agencies and selecting a list of five
- creating a current resume
- writing an introductory letter (Figure 1)

Before anyone begins an internship, realistic goals and expectations should be set and the following questions should be considered:

- How much time is reasonable to devote to the internship location?
- What are my exact responsibilities on the site?
- Do I understand the background and function of the agency?
- Do I understand my role as an intern?
- Do I realize the time commitment?
- Do I know the rules and regulations?
- Do I understand the consequences if I receive a poor evaluation or fail to complete the requirements?

Robert Smith
Chief of Police
Miami–Dade School Police
6100 N.W. 2nd Avenue
Miami, FL 33127

Dear Chief Smith:

As a student of criminal justice, I am interested in participating in Miami–Dade School Police Department's internship program. I have a particular interest in juvenile crime and I am also interested in law enforcement investigations and community policing.

My current schedule permits great flexibility on any assignments that may be associated with the internship. Please find enclosed my resume with references for your review.

I would like the opportunity to be considered for the internship program at Miami–Dade School Police Department and would be available for an interview at your convenience.

Very truly yours,

David Anderson

Figure 1

Evaluation and Completion

The successful completion of a criminal justice internship program may be critical to career opportunities. Internships provide not only experience but also references. Receiving a poor performance or negative evaluation from an internship not only may jeopardize future placements, but may also serve as a poor indicator of interest or ability to work in the criminal justice system.

Alpha Phi Sigma: The National Criminal Justice Honor Society

The purpose of Alpha Phi Sigma is to recognize and promote high scholarship among students actively engaged in collegiate preparation for professional services, to keep abreast of the advances in scientific research, to elevate the ethical standards of the criminal justice profession, and to establish in the public mind the benefit and necessity of education. Alpha Phi Sigma is the only nationally recognized honor society for the study of criminal justice that is fully accredited by the Association of College Honor Societies. Alpha Phi Sigma was created at Washington State University in 1942. In 1976, the Academy of Criminal Justice Sciences recognized Alpha Phi Sigma as the national criminal justice honor society and combined annual national conferences. Currently, Alpha Phi Sigma has 130 active chapters with an international membership of over 18,000. The organization includes four national officers, elected at the national conference, and four national criminal justice faculty advisors. Information on membership can be obtained from the National Secretariat at Alpha Phi Sigma National Secretariat, Florida International University, 3000 N.E. 145th Street, North Campus, North Miami, FL 33181.

CAREERS IN CRIMINAL JUSTICE AND ANCILLARY PROFESSIONS

Careers in Criminal Justice

The criminal justice system has three main components: courts, corrections, and law enforcement. An emerging strong ancillary profession is private security. The scope of this profession is far more extensive than the common perception of a bank guard. Almost every aspect of the criminal justice system has been affected by the privatization concept, a concept addressed later in this chapter.

Police Personnel

People who seek employment in the field of criminal justice are usually long-term employees. A study by the International Association of Chiefs of Police indicated that over 90% of the police officers surveyed planned to make law enforcement a life career. The same study showed that approximately 80% gave little to no thought to leaving police service (Radelet, 1986).

MIAMI POLICE DEPARTMENT 1998

Length of Police Service by Rank

Rank	Years of Service						
	0–4	5–9	10–14	15–19	20–24	25–29	30–over
Chief of police					1		
Deputy chief				2	2		
Major			3	2	7	2	
Captain				1	7	5	
Lieutenant			20	6	11	5	
Sergeant	2	15	49	11	58	7	1
Police officer	166	230	338	56	49	8	

SERVICE YEARS

Years	(%)
0–4	15.8
5–9	23.1
10–14	38.5
15–19	7.2
20–24	12.8
25–29	2.5
30–+	.1

(*Source:* Miami Police Department Annual Report, 1998.)

The annual report from the City of Miami Police Department also indicated that the average length of service of all law enforcement personnel is 12 years. They reported that only 3.8% of the total police department was less than 24 years of age, and about 4% was over the age of 59. Over 50% of the police personnel fall within the age group of 30 to 39.

Law Enforcement Salaries

In 1967, the President's Commission on Law Enforcement and the Administration of Justice recommended a starting salary for police officers to be between $7000 and $10,000. Currently, the police departments in Florida have a starting range from about $25,000 to $36,000, depending on geographical area and agency size. Most state and federal agencies fall within or close to these boundaries.

Federal Law Enforcement

Most federal agencies require a bachelor's degree for entry level employment, and some are setting minimum grade-point averages. The selection process usually takes several months after submission of the application and required documents. For more information, contact:

- Alcohol, Tobacco and Firearms Special Agent
  650 Massachusetts Avenue, S.W.
  Washington, D.C. 20226

- Customs Inspector/Special Agent
  1301 Constitution Avenue, N.W.
  Washington, D.C. 20229

- Drug Enforcement Administration (DEA) Agent
  United States Department of Justice
  Arlington, VA 22202

- Federal Bureau of Investigation (FBI) Agent
  9th Street and Pennsylvania Avenue, N.W.
  Washington, D.C. 20535

- Department of State
  Recruitment & Employment Division
  2201 C Street, N.W.
  Washington, D.C. 20520

- Capitol Police
  119 D Street, N.W.
  United States Capitol Building
  Washington, D.C. 20510

- Immigration and Naturalization Service
  425 I Street, N.W.
  Washington, D.C. 20536

- Internal Revenue Criminal Investigator
  1111 Constitution Avenue, N.W.
  Washington, D.C. 20224

- Naval Investigator Service
  Career Service Department
  Washington, D.C. 20415

- Postal Service Inspector
  9600 Newbridge Drive
  Potomac, MD 20858

- Secret Service Agent
  United States Treasury Department
  1800 G Street, N.W.
  Washington, D.C. 20223

- United States Marshal Service
  600 Army Navy Drive
  Arlington, VA 22202

- United States Park Police
  National Park Service
  1100 Ohio Drive, S.W.
  Washington, D.C. 20242

State of Florida Law Enforcement

For further information, contact:

- Florida Alcohol Beverage Control
  8685 N.W. 53 Terrace
  Miami, FL 33166

- Florida Department of Law Enforcement
  P.O. Box 1489
  Tallahassee, FL 32302

- Florida Highway Patrol
  3900 Apalachee Parkway
  Tallahassee, FL 32399

- Florida Marine Patrol
  P.O. Box 381906
  Miami, FL 33172

- Florida Fish and Game Commission
  3900 Commonwealth Blvd.
  Tallahassee, FL 32399

State of Florida University Police Departments

The following universities maintain their own police departments:

- Florida A & M University

- Florida Atlantic University

- Florida International University

- Florida State University

- University of Central Florida

- University of North Florida

- University of South Florida

- University of West Florida

- Gulf Coast University

- University of Florida

County Law Enforcement

Employment opportunities include investigators for the State's Attorney Offices or individual sheriff's departments (67 counties).

Local Law Enforcement

Positions are available at the 291 local police agencies.

Opportunities in the Court System

Positions include court bailiffs, court administrators, court clerks, pretrial officers, victim services, and domestic violence services.

Opportunities in Corrections

The Florida Department of Corrections recruits for Correctional Officers and Correctional Probation Officers throughout the State of Florida. The following are examples of the department's current qualifications and benefits:

- *Correctional officer:* Call toll-free 1-888-610-0603 for application information.

  - salary range: $20,109–$31,075 annually, with salary adjustments ranging from $3800.00 to $6300.00 annually for certain South Florida counties

- ➤ fully paid enhanced (special risk) retirement program

- ➤ $275 annual clothing and shoe allowance

- ➤ required to complete the basic recruit training course and successfully pass the Florida Officer Certification Examination; correctional officer applicants who have not completed basic recruit training may be hired in trainee status

- ➤ high school diploma or its equivalent (GED) required

- ➤ staff housing provided, when applicable

- ➤ step pay plan increases

- *Correctional probation officer:* Call toll-free 1-888-610-0602 for application information.

  - ➤ salary range $22,268–$35,777 annually, with salary adjustments of $4640 annually for certain South Florida counties.

  - ➤ Bachelor's degree required

  - ➤ Correctional probation officer applicants normally hired in trainee status until they have successfully passed basic recruit training and the Florida Officer Certification Exam

- Minimum qualifications for correctional officer and correctional probation officer:

  - ➤ 19 years old or older

  - ➤ United States citizen

  - ➤ not convicted of a felony or a misdemeanor involving perjury or a false statement

  - ➤ honorable discharge from any of the armed forces of the Unites States

  - ➤ good moral character as determined by a background investigation

  - ➤ physical examination and drug test successfully passed

- Benefits include:

  - ➤ criminal justice incentive pay up to $130 per month

  - ➤ promotional opportunities

  - ➤ 13 vacation days and 13 sick-leave days the first year

  - ➤ 10 paid holidays

  - ➤ fully paid retirement program

  - ➤ state-subsidized health insurance

  - ➤ state-subsidized life insurance

  - ➤ pre-tax medical and child-care benefits

  - ➤ supplemental insurance (car, dental, cancer, legal)

  - ➤ childcare facilities in some locations

Preferences are given to certain veterans, spouses of veterans, and minorities, as provided by the Florida Statutes. Physical and drug tests are required. Opportunities are also available in various medical and administrative careers. For additional information regarding opportunities within the Florida Department of Corrections, contact Florida Department of Corrections, Personnel, Attn: Recruitment Office Room 300, 2601 Blair Stone Road, Tallahassee, FL 32399-2500, (904) 488-3130 or SC 278-3130.

For additional opportunities within the corrections field, contact:

- The American Correctional Association
  8025 Laurel Lakes Court
  Laurel, MD 20707

- The Federal Prison Industries
  Central Office
  320 First Street, N.W.
  Washington, D.C. 20534

- Department of Corrections
  1311 Winewood Avenue
  Tallahassee, FL 32399

Correction Officer Local/State/Federal

Positions available include juvenile counselors; parole officers, state/federal; pre-release program services; and probation officers, state/federal.

Forensic Science

For further information, contact:

- Florida Department of Law Enforcement Labs
  Jacksonville: 711-A Liberty Street, Jacksonville, FL 32202
  Pensacola: 160 Governmental Center, Pensacola, FL 32501
  Tallahassee: 420 North Adams Street, Tallahassee, FL 32302
  Tampa: P.O. Box 151776, Tampa, FL 33684

- Broward County Crime Lab
  1500 Broward Boulevard
  Fort Lauderdale, FL 33312

- Drug Enforcement Administration
  5205 Northwest 84th Avenue
  Miami, FL 33166

- Metro–Miami–Dade Police Crime Lab
  9105 N.W. 25th Street
  Miami, FL 33172

- Palm Beach Sheriff's Crime Lab
  3228 Gun Club Road
  West Palm Beach, FL 22416

Ancillary Professions

The 1985 Hallcrest report indicated that improvement of private security in the overall safety and security of communities had not been fully realized. Outside of this report (Cunningham and Taylor, 1985; Cunningham et al., 1990), private criminal justice professions have received minimal analysis and limited scholarly attention. Private criminal justice professions are not limited to security personnel providing police or security service, but also encompass a wide spectrum of careers. The National Institute of Justice initiated a comprehensive study (conducted by the Hallcrest Systems, Inc., Portland, Oregon), to research the role and utilization of private security within the United States. The study concluded that expenditures for private security professions exceed $21 billion annually. The personnel involved in the industry outnumber public police by about two to one. The second of the Hallcrest reports (1990) estimated employment within the United States in private security at 1,493,300 persons, with a projected growth to over 1,900,000 by the year 2000 (Cunningham et al., 1990).

Growth Trends in Private Security

The trend of rapid growth is expected to continue. The development of private criminal justice professions may be partially attributed to the general public's perception that traditional criminal justice has failed to control crime. Disappointment in the criminal justice service and growing crime problems have resulted in innumerable special-interest groups that demand additional service in their communities. The development of intervention by citizens into public criminal justice may be an outgrowth of crime control concerns perpetuated by the news media and which may include the excessive costs of operating a criminal justice system, an operation that may not always be satisfactory to public concerns.

Reclassifications in Criminal Justice

Over the last decade, trends in criminal justice have changed. Public concerns have dictated that a significant number of public police assignments be distributed to the private sector. The reclassification of numerous tasks that have been historically held by police officers has changed the relationship between the public and private sectors. Examples include dispatching for police, fire, and emergency medical service; police telephone report reception; traffic accident investigation; computer centers; and crime analysis. Some reports have suggested a role for private security in the traditional service of patrolling neighborhoods.

Information on Private Security Careers

For information, contact:

- American Society of Industrial Security
  1655 North Fort Myers Drive
  Arlington, VA 22209

- National Fire Protection Association
  1 Batterymarch Park
  Quincy, MA 02269

- International Security Management Association
  P.O. Box 623
  Buffalo, IA 52728

- American Society of Safety Engineers
  850 Busse Highway
  Park Ridge, IL 60068

Opportunities in Private Security

Positions include institutional security, privatized correction facilities, industrial security, private investigations, railroad police, retail investigator, loss protection/prevention specialist, and private personal protection specialist.

Professional Organizations

Professional organizations include:

- Academy of Criminal Justice Sciences
  Northern Kentucky University
  402 Nun Hall
  Highland Heights, KY 41099

- International Association of Chiefs of Police
  1110 North Glebe Road
  Arlington, VA 22201

- National Organization of Black Law Enforcement Executives
  908 Pennsylvania Avenue
  Washington, D.C. 20003

- National Sheriff's Association
  1450 Duke Street
  Alexandria, VA 22314

- Southern Criminal Justice Association
  Spartanburg Methodist College
  1200 Textile Drive
  Spartanburg, SC 29301

THE CRIMINAL JUSTICE ENTRY PROCESS

The Application

Most criminal justice agencies have criteria that must be met before initiating the application process in regard to age, vision, education, possession of a driver's license, drug use, serious criminal convictions, and residency; however, some classifications of certain jobs have additional criteria. The style and format of the application will vary from agency to agency but most will require basic background information. The initial application is an important document in the hiring and selection process because the instrument will be used as a written foundation for the remaining process. Applicants must avoid the temptation to exaggerate qualifications. Distorting information on the application includes selectively listing past employers and failing to list traffic violations. Generally, these applications are scrutinized closely and dishonest candidates will most likely be eliminated.

The Written Exam

Most agencies require some form of written examination to measure basic intelligence. Generally, tests for employment within the criminal justice system are fundamentally education based. Test items generally include math (addition, subtraction, and multiplication), reading comprehension, and basic writing skills. With new state testing requirements for college graduation, some agencies are exempting candidates with college degrees from the entry-level test.

The Medical Exam

In an attempt to exclude people with existing health problems (e.g., problems with the heart, back, or knees) from work requirements that may exacerbate such problems, a medical examination is required. This examination is usually conducted by a physician and may vary from being very comprehensive to being a general physical examination.

The Psychological Examination

Because of the emphasis on agencies to minimize police and law enforcement use of force abuses, the psychological examination becomes very important in the screening process. The exam is constructed to determine the emotional and psychological stability of a candidate. The test is designed to identify individuals who have violent propensities or other traits undesirable to the criminal justice professional. The format for the test is usually developed in two parts; the first is a lengthy multiple-choice exam followed by an interview by a psychologist. Some agencies also require reexamination for reassignment to a stressful position.

The Polygraph Examination

Many agencies use the polygraph as a candidate screening tool. The polygraph or lie detector is touted by police agencies as an effective tool to uncover problems with some applicants (Swanson et al., 1993). The polygraph has been absorbed into contemporary technology and can be administered and analyzed via sophisticated computer software. The initial written application may be utilized as a base for the questions, along with inquiries about drug use, sale, and possession; criminal acts; and other behavior inappropriate for future members of the criminal justice system.

Physical Agility Test

Many agencies find it necessary to test candidates to determine their physical ability. The current test appears to have lowered the high physical standards that once allowed only the strongest persons to successfully pass and precluded others from completing the process. Today, most of the testing focuses on upper-body strength, leg strength, grip strength, balance and coordination, and quick reaction (Roberg and Kuykendall, 1990). Many agencies provide candidates with a full description of the testing events, with tips for successful completion, well in advance of the exam date.

The Oral Interview

The oral portion of the process provides the agency with an opportunity to evaluate the candidate's ability to communicate, to think clearly, and to organize thoughts, as well as observe general mannerisms. A candidate's attire for the interview is a part of the overall impression. The interviewing panel may consist of four or five people. This is a portion of the process that can be practiced before the interview. Questions such as "Why do you want to become a police officer?," "What are your strengths and weaknesses?," "What do you think causes problems in society?," and "What do you think can be done about crime?" are common. By utilizing a tape recorder a candidate can practice his responses.

Background Investigation

One of the last steps of the entry-level screening process is the applicant's background investigation. Depending on the thoroughness of the agency, the background investigation may include interviews with high school teachers, past and present employers, neighbors, and friends. The investigation may include a credit history, criminal history, traffic record, juvenile history, military service records, college transcripts, and family background information. It is important that the initial application information provided by the candidate matches information revealed by the investigation.

CONCLUSION

The criminal justice system provides a wealth of career opportunities. The traditional role of the local sworn police officer patrolling the streets has been broadened tremendously over the years. Now individuals have many employment options with a variety of federal, state, and local agencies. Federal agents include Alcohol, Tobacco, and Firearms special agents, customs inspectors, DEA agents, FBI agents, postal inspectors, Secret Service agents, U.S. Marshals, Internal Revenue criminal investigators, and capitol police. The State of Florida offers employment not only with the Florida Department of Law Enforcement, but also with the Alcohol Beverage Control, Florida Highway Patrol, Florida Marine Patrol, and Florida Fish and Game Commission.

Ancillary positions in the criminal justice system range from court bailiff to pretrial officer, victim services, court clerk, juvenile counselor, parole officer, probation officer, and forensic sciences. Additionally, the utilization of private security for institutional and industrial security, privatized correction facilities, private investigations, railroad police, retail investigations and loss protection/prevention have more than doubled the availability of positions within the field.

The entry-level employment process generally consists of a written employment application; written, medical, psychological, and polygraph examinations; a physical agility test; and an oral interview. A background investigation could be very extensive, depending on the agency's needs and thoroughness.

Education levels for criminal justice professionals vary from agency to agency, but the list of proponents of college education for local, state, and federal agencies is growing. Numerous advantages of college-educated police are being recognized, including fewer disciplinary action cases and a greater number of alternative solutions to problems encountered in the community.

DISCUSSION QUESTIONS

1. Discuss the value of a college education in the criminal justice profession.

2. What are the benefits of participating in a criminal justice internship?

3. Identify federal, state, county, and municipal employment positions.

4. Discuss the concept of criminal justice privatization.

5. Identify the steps associated with the criminal justice entry process.

REFERENCES

Cunningham, W. and T. H. Taylor. 1985. *Private Security and Police in America (The Hallcrest Report)*. Portland, Oreg.: Chanceller Press.

Cunningham, W. C., J. J. Strauchs, and C. W. VanMeter. 1990. *Private Security Trends 1970–2000 (The Hallcrest Report II)*. Stoneham, Mass.: Butterworth-Heinemann.

Davis v. City of Dallas, 777 F. 2d 205 (5th Cir. 1985), cert. denied 476 U.S. 1116, 1986.

Florida Department of Law Enforcement (FDLE). 1993. *Crime in Florida: Annual Report*. Tallahassee, Fla.: Florida Department of Law Enforcement.

Kappeler, V. E., A. D. Sapp, and D. L. Carter. 1990. *Police Officer Higher Education, Citizen Complaints and Departmental Rule Violations*. Mimeo, Mo.: Central Missouri State University.

Myren, R. A. 1982. A second view, in Joint Commission on Criminology and Criminal Justice Education and Standards, *Two Views of Criminology and Criminal Justice: Definition, Trends, and the Future*. Chicago: University of Chicago.

Radelet, L. A. 1986. *The Police and the Community*, 4th ed. New York: Macmillan.

Roberg, R. R. and J. Kuykendall. 1990. *Police Organization and Management: Behavior, Theory, and Processes*. Pacific Grove, Calif.: Brooks/Cole Publishing.

Sherman, L. W. and the National Advisory Commission on Higher Education for Police Officers. 1978. *The Quality of Police Education*. San Francisco, Calif.: Jossey-Bass.

Steward, J. 1985. Public safety and private police, *Public Administration Review*, November, pp. 758–765.

CHAPTER 8

The Florida Correctional System

CHAPTER OVERVIEW

This chapter reviews the Florida correctional system from its fledgling beginning in Chattahoochee in the 1800s with 82 prisoners to its current, overburdened status of being the fourth largest prison system in the United States, with an inmate population of over 71,233. The Florida chain gangs as well as two models for prison systems are discussed. Steps of an inmate are traced through the correctional system from presentence investigation to death row. Additional topics include the costs of incarceration, prisoners' deprivations in prison, demographics of the inmate population, medical and counseling treatment, gaintime, escapes, and crimes in prison. Boot camps, home confinement, and electronic monitoring are discussed as alternatives to incarceration. The breakdown of the 133 locations in Florida for incarceration is provided in terms of types and quantities of facilities, as well as the population in each.

HISTORICAL VIEW

The State of Florida was associated with the South during the Civil War and its penological views were consistent with southern prison systems. Overcrowding, chaining, hard labor, and brutality were common as the southern style of treating inmates. After the Civil War and during the years that Florida was enduring reconstruction, enterprising politicians developed a system to lease prisoners to private construction companies as hard laborers for $100 per year per prisoner. The arsenal at Chattahoochee was used for a state prison and had 82 prisoners in the late 1800s. Because prison management was not a major concern at the time, this system minimized the cost of prison operations. As Florida evolved under influence from northern developers and politicians, this system was replaced with a prison system similar to the northern states (McKelvey, 1977).

THE CONGREGATE AND SEGREGATE SYSTEMS

Early in the 1800s, two models for prisons began to develop: the *segregate,* or Pennsylvania, system and the *congregate,* or Auburn, system. The segregate model emphasized complete isolation of inmates. Prisoners were kept in individual cells most of the time and they were never allowed to interact with other inmates. In contrast, the congregate system permitted interaction with others, including working in groups; however, this system prohibited inmates from talking with one another. Both systems had their supporters and critics (Travis, 1990).

THE FLORIDA CHAIN GANG

From the concept of the prisoner lease system emerged the chain-gang system. This program provided work crews for labor outside the prison facility, mostly for public projects, cleaning storm drains, picking up trash along highways, and other labor-intensive jobs. Florida abolished the chain-gang system in the late 1940s. Some states, including Florida, are revisiting the chain gang program and are considering reestablishing this type of prison labor. Florida has grown from the 82 inmates housed at Chattahoochee into the fourth largest prison system in the United States.

PRESENTENCE INVESTIGATION

In most cases, after conviction, the probation department performs a presentence investigation. The investigation report outlines the crime committed and the offender's history, both as a criminal and as a citizen. The victim's statement may be part of the document package presented to the judge. Usually, the defendant does not have the opportunity to review the presentencing package; however, in *Gardner v. Florida,* 430 U.S. 349, 1977 (a death penalty case), the court indicated that information contained in the report influenced the penalty. Therefore, in cases that are subject to the death penalty, defendants may request an examination of such document.

PUNISHMENT AND SENTENCING

Theories of punishment are numerous and vary according to society and political philosophies, but they will not be reiterated at this time. Instead, it is important here to focus on the generally acknowledged four goals of punishment: retribution, deterrence (general and specific), incapacitation, and rehabilitation (see table). The Florida Department of Corrections utilizes various methods that fall within these goals but also fall outside the use of incarceration alone.

GOALS OF PUNISHMENT

1. *Retribution:* Punishment of a person who has committed a crime and deserves the sanctions imposed. The basic objective simply implies that a person who harms another deserves to be harmed.

2a. *Deterrence (general):* The punishment of offenders sets an example to the general public that people are apprehended and sanctioned for criminal acts. This in turn discourages community members from attempting crimes.

2b. *Deterrence (specific):* The punishment of offenders discourages them from engaging in criminal behavior in the future.

3. *Incapacitation:* Punishment by incarceration (in prison) prevents the offender from committing crimes against society.

4. *Rehabilitation:* Through vocational training, counseling, education, or other means of corrective behavior, the offender can emerge as a contributor to society.

CONCURRENT AND CONSECUTIVE SENTENCES

In some cases where several crimes have been committed with subsequent convictions, the offender may receive a *concurrent* sentence. This requires the person to serve the longest sentence while serving the other shorter sentences at the same time. For example, a person is convicted of burglary of a home, robbery of the resident, and then stealing a vehicle. The sentence is 5 years for the burglary, 7 years for the robbery, and 3 years for the auto theft, to be served concurrently. This inmate would be released in 7 years.

Cases that involve *consecutive* sentencing require the person to serve out each individual sentence before starting another. For example, in the case where the sentence for a conviction of burglary is 5 years, conviction of robbery is 7 years, and conviction of auto theft is 3 years, the individual would be required to serve 15 years in the state prison.

ENTERING THE PRISON SYSTEM

Every person who is sentenced to the state prison system is required to undergo a complete assessment to determine violent propensities, risk of escape, and any special needs of the inmate. Prisoners convicted of murder, manslaughter, sexual offenses, robbery, aggravated assault, or other violent crimes are of particular concern during the evaluation process. In 1994/95, over 22,000 inmates were assessed and placed. Florida also utilizes the client management classification system. This system separates the inmates into patterns of behavior and attitude, based on five indicators. Each indicator predicts both positive and negative behavior.

DEPRIVATIONS IN FLORIDA STATE PRISON

Sykes (1969) identified five areas of distress that inmates experience related to incarceration:

- *Deprivation of liberty*—Once incarcerated within the prison, a person's freedom of movement is eliminated. The freedom of choice involving eating, associating, exercising, etc. is lost.

- *Deprivation of goods and services*—Civilian clothing, jewelry, and money are confiscated. Inmates no longer have the ability to dine at restaurants, shop at malls, and attend community events.

- *Deprivation of heterosexual relations*—Most of Florida's prisons are segregated by sex. The absence of opposite-sex contact leads to anxieties about sexual identity among inmates. The effect is both physical and psychological.

- *Deprivation of autonomy*—The state prison provides and decides for all inmates. Prisoners lose the mental thought process associated with decision making. Because decisions regarding where to go, when and what to eat, what to wear, and where to work are made by prison authorities, inmates lose their autonomy.

- *Deprivation of security*—State prison is not necessarily a safe and secure place to reside; 1724 assaults in Florida State prison system occurred in 1995. The prison community is a population of people with violent behavioral problems and people with an inability to compromise peacefully. Prison life is stressful, frightening, and at times dangerous.

INMATE POPULATION

Over the last decade the population of prisons in the State of Florida has increased from approximately 28,000 to over 71,233. Of the 71,233 inmates, blacks account for 54.3% (38,679), whites account for 43.4% (30,894), and about 2% are classified as other. The male population is about 58,000, of whom, 54.3% are black and under 29 years of age.

INMATE STATS

Typical Admission

Male (91.2%)
Black (53.9%)
29 or younger (52.2%)

Prison Sentence of

4 years or less (60.7%)

Convicted of

Drug sale (13.1%)
Burglary (8.5%)
Drug possession (8.1%)

Convicted in

Miami–Dade County (13.8%)
Broward County (13.7%)
Hillsborough County (10.0%)

DRUG OFFENDER CONVICTIONS

Typical Drug Offender

Black (71.2%)
31 or younger (51.5%)

Prison Sentence of

3 years or less (64.4%)

Convicted of

Sale/manufacture (52.0%)
Possession (32.2%)
Trafficking (15.8%)

Convicted in

Miami–Dade County (14.3%)
Broward County (20.1%)
Hillsborough County (11.3%)

FEMALE OFFENDER CONVICTIONS

Typical Female Offender

Black (52.1%)
31 or younger (55.0%)

Prison Sentence of

3 years or less (60.2%)

Convicted of

Drug sale (16.7%)
Drug possession (16.3%)
Grand theft (7.6%)

Convicted in

Miami–Dade County (11.5%)
Broward County (14.4%)
Hillsborough County (10.8%)

FEMALE OFFENDERS BY RACE

Race	Number	Percentage
White	1587	43.7
Black	1894	52.1
Other	152	4.2
Totals	3633	100

Female Primary Offenses

Crime	Number	Percentage
Murder	578	15.9
Sex offense	42	1.2
Robbery	304	8.4
Violence	583	16.0
Burglary	395	10.9
Property crime	517	14.2
Drugs	1061	29.2
Weapons	44	1.2
Other offenses	109	3.0
Totals	3633	100

(*Source:* Florida Department of Corrections, 1990–1995.)

FLORIDA'S FEMALE OFFENDERS

The 1998/1999 Florida Correctional Report indicated that females represent almost 6% of the total offender population. Female offenders bring unique problems to the correctional facility. Approximately 80% of the women in prison are mothers, the majority of whom are single caretakers of minor children prior to incarceration. Many are immature and lack self-esteem and child-raising skills; however, data indicate that over 90% of female offenders are released and returned to their originating communities. The Department of Corrections has instituted the Female Offender Plan to assist female inmates in becoming more self-reliant, thus reducing recidivism (repeat offenses).

Priority Issues for the Female Offender Plan

- Ensure that the specific needs of female offenders are met.

- Develop programs and services that assist in personal growth, gaining maturity, and reintegrating successfully into society.

- Develop vocational and job-related skills to support economic freedom.

- Address the physiological, psychological, and substance abuse needs.

COUNSELING AND EMPLOYMENT TRAINING PROGRAMS

Persons sentenced to state prison enter through one of five intake centers where they are tested and classified. Inmates are grouped in relationship to educational needs, medical requirements, labor skills, and security risks. Inmates who are identified as in need of, and receptive to, substance abuse counseling are assigned to appropriate programs. Others are placed in various positions within the prison community. State-prison-based industries include agriculture, furniture building, clothing, state license plates, and other related tasks. Since 1984, prison industries have been operated by Prison Rehabilitative Industries and Diversified Enterprises (PRIDE) as a non-profit corporation.

MEDICAL TREATMENT IN PRISON

Under mandate by the federal government, state prisons are required to provide health services at the community's standard level. Emergency medical care as well as health education are provided. One of the more serious medical issues in the correctional facility is the response to AIDS. Diagnosing and preventing the spread of AIDS among inmates is a priority of prison medical personnel. In 1976, the U.S. Supreme Court clarified prisoners' rights to proper medical care. In *Estelle v. Gamble,* the court created the following standard:

> Deliberate indifference to serious medical needs of prisoners constitutes the unnecessary and wanton infliction of pain, proscribed by the Eighth Amendment. This is true whether the indifference is manifested by prison doctors in their response to the prisoner's needs or by prison guards in intentionally denying or delaying access to medical care or intentionally interfering with the treatment once prescribed. (429 U.S. 97, 97 S. Ct. 285, 50 L.Ed.2d 251, 1976)

GAINTIME

Prior to October 1, 1995

Gaintime, also termed *good behavior time,* is a system to encourage inmates to behave in a proper manner while incarcerated. The system rewards prisoners with a reduction in time off their sentence. Florida has used the gaintime system for controlling inmates since 1889 and has developed five types of awards (Florida Department of Corrections):

- *Basic gaintime* (F.S. 944.275) was eliminated as part of the Safe Streets Act of 1992–93, which eliminated basic gaintime for all inmates who committed crimes on or after

January 1, 1994, and are subsequently sentenced to prison. Previously, inmates sentenced for offenses committed after July 1, 1978, received 10 days of basic gaintime for each month of sentence imposed. Inmates serving life or certain minimum/mandatory sentences are not eligible, regardless of their offense date.

- *Incentive gaintime* (F.S. 944.275(4)(b)) is awarded to inmates for adjustment, work, and participation in programs. The awards are made on a monthly basis as earned (unless prohibited by law), and the amount of the time awarded varies in relation to the inmate's rated performance and adjustment. Inmates who commit crimes on or after January 1, 1994, may earn up to 25 days of incentive gaintime per month if the crime of conviction falls within levels one through seven of the revised sentencing guidelines. If the crime of conviction falls within levels eight to ten, or the crime was committed after 1983 but before January 1, 1994, the inmate is only eligible for up to 20 days per month of gaintime.

- *Meritorious gaintime* (F.S. 944.275(4)(c)) may be awarded to an inmate for an outstanding deed. The maximum award is 60 days.

- *Educational achievement gaintime* (F.S. 944.275(4)(d)) may be awarded to an inmate who receives a General Education Development (GED) diploma or a certificate for completion of a vocational program. The inmate can receive a one-time award of 60 days.

- *Educational gaintime* (F.S. 944.275(2)(e)) may be awarded to an inmate who satisfactorily completes the Mandatory Literacy program, as determined by the institution's educational program manager. It is a one-time award of 6 days.

After October 1, 1995

Sentences for criminal offenses committed on or before October 1, 1995, do not permit gaintime for inmates. Persons committing crimes are now required to serve a minimum of 85% of their sentences. Any inmate in prison prior to October 1, 1995, does not fall into this requirement; however, it is now difficult to cut substantial time from a sentence. The Department of Corrections reported that the average percentage of sentences served by inmates released in June 1997 was 71%, as compared to only 34% 5 years ago.

THE FACILITIES

Florida has 133 locations in which those convicted of a crime can serve their sentences. The system has five regions (with the central office located in Tallahassee) 51 major institutions, 32 community correctional centers, 5 road prisons, 11 stand-alone work/forestry camps and drug treatment centers, 27 work camps, and 7 contract drug treatment centers.

FLORIDA PRISONS

	Facilities	Facilities (Male)	Facilities (Female)	Facilities (Male and Female)	Population
Major institutions	51	46	4	1	50,171
Community centers	32	24	8	—	2616
Road prisons	5	5	0	—	315
Forestry/drug centers	11	10	1	—	1587
Work camps	27	27	0	—	6697
Contract drug centers	7	1	1	5	470

(*Source:* Florida Department of Corrections, 1990–1995.)

PRISON AMENITIES

Work in Prison

About 83% of all inmates participate in work programs, vocational training, or academic classes. Inmate labor is used for the construction of new prisons, preparing meals, maintenance, sanitation, farming, and recycling programs.

Television

Currently, no correctional facilities provide cable or satellite television entertainment. Most prisons have basic television reception for recreational use; however, a recent state law prohibits the use of public money (prison budgets) for the purchase of recreational television.

Air-Conditioning

Of the 55 major state-managed prisons, only seven have air-conditioning: Brevard, Broward, Miami–Dade, Hillsborough, Lancaster, and Union counties and the Corrections Mental Health Institution. Prisons that were constructed under the privatization contract are all air-conditioned.

CRIMES IN PRISON

The disciplinary reports written by Florida Department of Corrections employees exceeded 68,144 for 1999 to 2000. Serious crime continues to grow within the prison population. One explanation for this growth may result from the diversionary programs developed by the courts for nonviolent offenders, as only the more violent criminals are incarcerated within the prison system.

FLORIDA DEPARTMENT OF CORRECTIONS DISCIPLINARY FELONY REPORTS

Fiscal Year	Assaults	Fights	Contraband	Total Disciplinary Reports
1990/91	106	87	126	1156
1991/92	102	80	128	1165
1992/93	106	76	133	1143
1993/94	111	84	150	1270

(*Source:* Florida Department of Corrections, 1990–1995.)

ASSAULTS ON STAFF AND INMATES

Fiscal Year	Assaults on Staff	Assaults on Inmates
1990/91	580	1499
1991/92	745	1284
1992/93	827	1367
1993/94	945	1769
1994/95	1116	1724

(*Source:* Florida Department of Corrections, 1990–1995.)

COST OF INCARCERATION

The cost for housing people in the Florida state prison system depends on the type of institution; however, the average cost to incarcerate a male inmate is about $40 per day or $14,600 a year. To incarcerate a youthful offender or juvenile inmate, the cost per day is estimated at $47 or $17,155 per year. The cost to incarcerate a female inmate is the highest, at about $50 per day or $18,250 per year. The Florida Department of Corrections employs more than 25,885 people and operates a budget of $1.5 billion.

FLORIDA PRISON COSTS

1990/91	1991/92	1992/93	1993/94	1994/95
$874,224,537	$907,372,474	$951,069,674	$1,034,257,832	$1,135,560,840

(*Source*: Florida Department of Corrections, 1990–1995.)

THE DEATH PENALTY

In June 1992, the U.S. Supreme Court decided that the death penalty was unconstitutional in *Furman v. Georgia.* In 1976, in the case of *Gregg v. Georgia,* the Court overturned the 1972 decision and allowed Florida to resume executions. In 1979, John Spenkelink became the first of 51 people to reside in a death row cell.

Death Row

The five methods of execution used in the United States are lethal injection, electrocution, lethal gas, hanging, and the firing squad. Currently, Florida uses two methods of execution: the electric chair and lethal injection. In 1932, the U.S. Legislature gave the State of Florida authority to execute inmates. In 1933, Florida conducted its first execution. In 1995, 352 inmates were on death row, including six women. Males awaiting execution are incarcerated at Union Correctional Institution and Florida State Prison in Starke. Females awaiting execution are incarcerated at Broward Correctional Institution in Pembroke Pines. The entire execution process takes about 10 minutes and is conducted by an anonymous private citizen (not a corrections officer) who is paid $175.00 per execution.

Death Watch

The death watch cell at Florida State Prison is larger than the traditional cell. The structure is 12 × 7 × 8.5 feet and has a continuous watch. The evening prior to execution, an inmate may request a special last meal, excluding alcohol. If the request cannot be made in the prison kitchen, it can be purchased locally; however, the total cost cannot exceed $20.

The Execution

Electrocutions of inmates take place at Florida State Prison. Several accounts have been recorded by witnesses of a Florida execution. Usually, 12 civilian witnesses, one physician, and a number of prison officials are present during the actual electrocution. The electric chair is a large, three-legged, oak structure. The door at the back of the room that houses the electric chair leads to the death watch cell. This is the corridor down which the condemned person walks to reach the electrocution room. Prior to execution, the condemned person's head is shaved and covered with electrolytic gel. Additionally, the right leg is prepared in the same manner. Correction officers strap the person to the chair, utilizing leg, arm, wrist, and chest straps. After the condemned person has an opportunity to make a statement, a black headpiece with leather mask is fitted into place to obscure the inmate's face from witnesses looking through the window. With an indication from the superintendent of Florida State Prison, the executioner sends 2000 volts and 14 amps flowing through the inmate's body. A 2-minute automatic cycle of 2000 volts completes this process. Once death is confirmed by the attending physician, the superintendent announces to the witnesses, "The sentence of the State of Florida vs. [name of the inmate] has been carried out at [time of death]." The entire process consumes less than 10 minutes.

Lethal Injection

The inmate is accompanied from the holding cell to the execution room and placed on a gurney. His ankles and wrists are secured with restraints. A cardiac monitor and stethoscope are attached. Two saline intravenous lines are inserted, one in each arm. The witnesses are assembled, and the inmate is given an opportunity to make a statement. At the conclusion of the inmate's statement, the warden gives the order to proceed. A curtain is drawn and a sequence of three drug injections begins. First, a lethal dose of sodium thiopental is administered to render the inmate unconscious within about 30 seconds. Next, a substantial quantity of pancuronium bromide is given to collapse the diaphragm and lungs within about 45 seconds. The third lethal injection of potassium chloride stops the heart in about 30 seconds. The entire process takes less than 2 minutes. A physician examines the inmate, pronounces the death, and signs the death certificate. The estimated elapse time from restraint to death is about 17 minutes.

Inmate Insight

- The average length of stay on death row prior to execution is 11.3 years.

- The average age at the time of committing a death penalty offense is 30 years.

- The average age of a death row inmate is 40 years.

- The average age at the time of execution is 42 years.

ESCAPES FROM PRISON

In fiscal year 1999/2000, the Florida prison system experienced 87 escapes. Prisoner escapes have been dramatically reduced over the last 5 years. The majority of inmate escapes have been from community correctional centers and drug treatment centers, with the highest number of escapes taking place during the months of August and May. Over 82% of escapees are recaptured and reclassified.

PRISON ESCAPES

1995/1996	276
1996/1997	191
1997/1998	163
1998/1999	160
1999/2000	87

(*Source:* Florida Department of Corrections, 2001.)

COUNTY JAILS

Prisons are distinguishable from jails by the duration and seriousness of inmate convictions. A felony is a crime with a possible punishment of death or imprisonment in the state prison system for a period of one year or more. A misdemeanor is a crime less serious than a felony, with a possible punishment of less than one year in jail. The Florida Department of Corrections acts as a regulatory agency for the 67 county jails, of which 21 have multiple facilities. The state provides assistance and coordination, approves jail construction, and develops standards.

GROWTH OF THE COUNTY JAIL POPULATION

Year	Daily Population
1986	21,036
1987	24,602
1988	28,977
1989	33,050
1990	33,628
1991	34,766
1992	35,330
1993	34,530
1994	37,485

(*Source:* Florida Department of Corrections, 1990–1995.)

HOUSE CONFINEMENT AND ELECTRONIC MONITORING

House confinement is part of the Community Control Program, which has over 15,000 admissions. This type of program is usually imposed by the court and is not part of the prison system. In the majority of cases, the offenders are required to be confined to their place of residence at all times. Subjects under this type of confinement are only permitted to leave the residence during employment hours, imposed community service time, medical treatment, or under special conditions approved by the monitor supervisor. The technology of electronic monitors is computer programmed and continuously verifies the confinement of a person. Electronic monitoring equipment has several types of applications. One style utilizes a tamper-proof transmitter that is affixed to an ankle or wrist and sends an encoded signal at regular intervals to a receiver–dialer located in the home. Any disruption of that signal is reported by the receiver–dialer to the central computer. Disruptions are compared with the authorized leave schedule, and, as necessary, a violation is reported to the correctional staff.

BOOT CAMP

Boot camp incarceration presents a structured environment for those participating in the program. Many of the techniques and strategies of a strict military induction center are incorporated. Discipline, physical labor and punishment seem to be the common ingredient in most programs. Clear and Cole (1994) defined *boot camp* as a physically rigorous, disciplined, and demanding regimen emphasizing conditioning, education, and job training. This program is designed for young offenders. Several boot camp programs in Florida have been criticized for their failure to reduce recidivism rates.

THE FLORIDA PAROLE COMMISSION

This seven-member commission is appointed by the governor and cabinet and requires confirmation from the Senate. Established in 1941, the board serves as the control release authority of the state. The commission deals with matters that concern inmate release, including parole, emergency release, medical release, clemency, and full pardons. Contact:

Central Office Florida Department of Corrections

Michael Moore, Secretary
2601 Blair Stone Road
Tallahassee, FL 32399–2500
(904) 488-5021

CONCLUSION

Many forms of incarceration are available to the Florida Department of Corrections. These options range from the type of facility to the form of supervision. Within Florida an inmate can be housed in a prison, jail, community center, road prison, forestry or drug center, work camp, boot camp, contract drug center, or personal residence. The type of incarceration depends upon the individual's offense, age, violent propensities, risk of escape, and any special needs.

The inmate population has grown from 82 in the 1800s to over 71,233 in 2000. Of the current population, the typical admission is male (91.2%), black (53.9%), and 29 years of age or younger (52.2%). From 1993 to 1994, over 67,700 disciplinary reports were written by corrections department employees, of which 1270 were disciplinary felony reports. Assaults on correctional employees have more than doubled to 1116 from 1990/91 to 1994/95, while assaults on inmates have risen from 1499 to 1724 during the same period.

The cost to incarcerate an inmate in the State of Florida ranges from $40 to $50 a day depending on the age and sex of the inmate. The annual budget of the Florida Department of Corrections is approximately $1.5 billion, and it employs over 25,885 personnel.

Approximately 82% of the 308 escapees from the Florida prison system in 1994/95 were recaptured. The majority of these escapes occurred from community correctional centers and drug treatment centers, with the highest number of escapes occurring during the months of May and August.

DISCUSSION QUESTIONS

1. Discuss the congregate and segregate correctional systems.

2. Identify and discuss the four goals of punishment.

3. Discuss the five identified deprivations of prison life inmates experience.

4. How do inmates obtain gaintime?

5. Identify the five types of executions used in the United States.

PRISON TERMINOLOGY

Boot camp—A physically rigorous, disciplined, and demanding regimen emphasizing conditioning, education, and job training; designed for young offenders.

Capital punishment—Punishment of the convicted offender by death.

Career criminal—A person for whom crime is a way of earning a living. Over time, the career criminal has numerous contacts with the justice system and may come to look upon the criminal justice sanction as a normal business expense.

Classification—A process by which prisoners are assigned to types of custody and treatment appropriate to their individual needs.

Community correctional center—A small-group living facility for offenders, especially those who recently have been released from prison.

Community corrections—A model of corrections based on the assumption that the reintegration of the offender into the community should be the goal of the criminal justice system.

Conditions of release—Restrictions on a parolee's conduct that must be obeyed as a legally binding requirement of being released.

Congregate system—A penitentiary system developed in Auburn, New York, where each inmate was held in isolation during the night but worked with fellow prisoners during the day under a rule of silence.

Corrections—The variety of programs, services, facilities, and organizations responsible for the management of people who have been accused or convicted of criminal offenses.

Custodial model—A model of a correctional institution that emphasized security, discipline, and order.

Discretionary release—The release of an inmate from incarceration to community supervision at the discretion of the parole board within the boundaries set by the sentence and the penal law.

Diversion—An alternative to adjudication by which the defendant agrees to conditions set by the prosecutor (such as to undergo counseling or drug rehabilitation) in exchange for withdrawal of charges.

Due process (procedural)—The constitutional guarantee that no agent or instrumentality of government will use any procedures to arrest, prosecute, try, or punish any person other than those procedures prescribed by law.

False positive—An individual incorrectly classified because of imperfections in the method used.

Gaintime/good time—A reduction of time to be served in a correctional institution awarded at the discretion of correctional officials to inmates whose behavior conforms to the rules or whose activities deserve to be rewarded.

Jail—A facility authorized to hold pretrial detainees and sentenced misdemeanants for periods under one year. Most jails are administered by the County Sheriff.

Lease system—A variation on the piece-price system in which the contractor provided prisoners with food and clothing as well as raw materials. In Florida, under this system, prisoners were leased for labor.

Mandatory sentence—A sentence required by statute to be imposed and executed upon certain offenders.

Pardon—An action of the executive branch of state or federal government excusing an offense and absolving the offender from the consequences of the crime.

Parole—The conditional release of an inmate from incarceration under supervision after a portion of the prison sentence has been served.

Presentence investigation (PSI)—An investigation and summary report of the background of a convicted offender, prepared to help the judge decide on an appropriate sentence.

Prison—An institution for the imprisonment of persons convicted of felony crimes.

Recidivism—The repetition of crime by an offender.

Rehabilitation—The process of restoring a convicted offender to a constructive place in society through some form of vocational, educational, or therapeutic treatment.

Work release—Release of a sentenced inmate from a correctional institution for work during the day; the inmate must spend nights and weekends in the facility.

REFERENCES

Allen, H. E. and C. E. Simonsen. 1995. *Corrections in America: An Introduction.* Englewood Cliffs, N.J.: Prentice Hall.

Clear, T. R. and G. F. Cole. 1994. *American Corrections,* 3rd ed. Belmont, Calif.: Wadsworth Publishing.

Cromwell, P. F., Jr. and G. G. Killinger. 1994. *Community-Based Corrections: Probation, Parole, and Intermediate Sanctions.* New York: West Publishing.

Ferdico, J. N. (1992). *Criminal Law and Justice Dictionary.* St. Paul, Minn.: West Publishing.

Florida Criminal Law and Motor Vehicle Handbook. 1996. Longwood, Fla.: Gould Publications.

Florida Department of Corrections. 1990–1995. *Annual Reports.* Tallahassee, Fla.: State of Florida.

Fox, V. 1972. *Introduction to Corrections.* Englewood Cliffs, N.J.: Prentice-Hall.

Johnson, R. 1996. *Hard Time: Understanding and Reforming the Prison.* Belmont, Calif.: Wadsworth Publishing.

McKelvey, B. 1977. *American Prisons: A History of Good Intentions.* Montclair, N.J.: Patterson Smith.

Roberson, C. (1994). *Introduction to Criminal Justice.* Placerville, Calif.: Cooperhouse Publishing.

Senna, J. J. and L. J. Siegel. 1990. *Introduction to Criminal Justice,* 5th ed. St. Paul, Minn.: West Publishing.

Sykes, G. 1969. *The Society of Captives.* Princeton, N.J.: Princeton University Press.

Travis, L. F. III. 1990. *Introduction to Criminal Justice.* Cincinnati, Ohio: Anderson Publishing.

CHAPTER 9

The Florida Juvenile Justice System

CHAPTER OVERVIEW

The need to address juveniles differently from adults within the criminal justice system is discussed in this chapter. Reasons for this differentiation and methods of treating juveniles are provided for examination. Juvenile curfews, boot camps designed specifically for the youthful offender, and the Office of Youthful Offenders are examined. Statistics show that the crimes at public schools, and within the community as a whole, committed by juveniles are increasing at an alarming rate. This chapter examines statistics reflecting this increase, as well as the history of treatment of juveniles within the criminal justice system prior to the 20th century.

JUVENILE DELINQUENCY

Definitions

The State of Florida defines a juvenile as a person under the age of 18. This definition is consistent with 37 other states, the District of Columbia, and the federal courts. Some states view juveniles as people 15 years of age or younger, while others view them as being 17 years of age or younger. Federal law defines a juvenile delinquent as a person who has not reached his 18th birthday and violates any law of the U.S. Code. The violation would be considered a crime if committed by an adult (18 U.S.C. Section 5031, 1977).

Juvenile Court Design

Before the 20th century there was little difference between the treatment of a juvenile offender and an adult. Not until about 1900 did society recognize a need for different court systems. In 1905, in the case of *Commonwealth v. Fisher* (Pennsylvania Supreme Court), the court ruled *parens patriae,* which means the state could act as the parent. This philosophy also indicated that a delinquent was not considered a criminal.

The position of the courts changed in 1966 when the U.S. Supreme Court ruled in *Kent v. United States* (383 U.S. 541). This case clarified issues dealing with waivers or transfers to adult criminal court. A juvenile being considered for prosecution in criminal court has the right to counsel, the right to a hearing, and a statement of reasons for the transfer.

The Juvenile Delinquency Problem

The U.S. Justice Department (1995) reported that the frequency of juvenile arrests for violent crimes would double by the year 2010. The report reviewed arrest data between 1983 and 1992 and concluded that juvenile apprehensions increased 100%. Homicides committed by juveniles between 1984 and 1994 tripled (see figure).

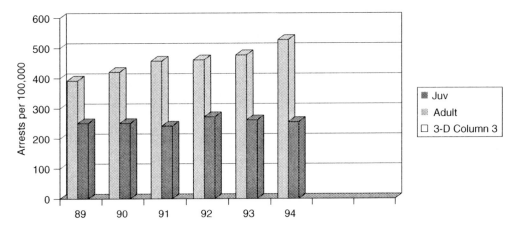

(*Source:* Office of Juvenile Justice and Delinquency, U.S. Bureau of the Census, 1995.)

The Office of Juvenile Justice reported that in 1994 handguns were used in two-thirds of all murders of juveniles. In 1994, 52% of all juvenile victims of homicide were black, and 61% of all juveniles arrested for homicide were black. The Uniform Crime Report indicates a relationship between age and crime and age and victimization. It appears that violent behavior peaks at about 18 years of age, and teenagers are about ten times more likely to be victimized than the elderly.

Juvenile Crime in Florida

Florida has significantly increased financial resources for the juvenile justice system since 1994. The 1994 budget for the juvenile system was $272 million, compared to $720 million in 1999. Corresponding to this increase, the delinquency rate declined from 7760 per 100,000 to 6750 per 100,000.

JUVENILE JUSTICE OVERVIEW

	Year				
	1992/93	1993/94	1994/95	1995/96	1996/97
Total juvenile population	1,266,107	1,306,326	1,309,126	1,361,544	1,413,367
Convictions					
Murder	162	161	158	106	101
Attempted murder	274	277	235	203	179
Armed robbery	1640	1671	1655	1300	1356
Aggravated assault	7326	8048	8549	8406	8936
Burglary	20,949	21,155	20,633	19,726	18,478
Auto theft	7669	8132	6997	5610	5373
Marijuana felony	619	930	1145	1214	1272
Marijuana misdemeanor	1997	3250	4110	4728	5288
Number of cases committed to adult court	6285	8079	9249	10,062	11,106
Bed capacity	2841	4278	5246	6038	7584
Budget	$197,144,760	$269,576,452	$383,411,880	$429,706,437	$480,920,654

According to the *Kids Count Data Book* (1995), a ranking of states in regard to safety for children, Florida ranked 48th. Only Tennessee, Mississippi, Louisiana, and Washington, D.C., ranked worse in the survey. The report also indicated a 57% increase in the number of juveniles arrested for violent crimes. In Miami–Dade County, police arrested 21,200 juveniles in 1994. The Miami–Dade County School Police reported over 3000 serious crimes committed within the 27 major high schools during the 1995/96 academic year.

Florida Juvenile Gangs

Juvenile gangs exist primarily in urban areas in this country, and Florida's cities are fertile areas for gang development. Contributing factors that cultivate gang activity include urbanization, rapid population growth, and ethnic and economic diversity. In 1995, the Florida Association of Sheriffs' Survey identified 380 juvenile gangs, with membership exceeding 11,000. Approximately two-thirds of the 32 contributing jurisdictions indicated that gang activity was a serious problem in their counties. Miami, Jacksonville, Orlando, and Tampa appeared to have the highest concentration of gang-related crime problems.

The Office of Juvenile Justice and Delinquency Prevention proposed the following guidelines (IDENTIFY) for authorities to engage in a proactive approach to juvenile gang activity:

> *Identify the problem:* Specify the problem and target location. Determine who is creating the problem, the specific nature of these activities, and where and when the problem is most intense.
>
> *Define the system components:* Determine which agencies in the community own the problem and have the authority and responsibility for solving it.
>
> *Enumerate policies, procedures, practices, programs, and resources*: Specify the existing agency policies and practices that address the problem and resources that are or could be used to address the problem.
>
> *Needs clarification:* Compare information on the nature and extent of the problem with existing resources to determine additional policy, procedures, practices, and program and resource needs.
>
> *Target strategies:* Identify the policies, procedures, practices, and programs and integrate them into a coordinated strategy to respond to the problem.
>
> *Implementation plan:* Prepare a plan that defines the objectives, tasks, and resources to be dedicated by each participating agency for implementing the strategy.
>
> *Focus agency responsibilities:* Identify the specific activities of the strategy to be performed by each participating agency, define the role and responsibilities of each agency in implementing the activities, and ensure accountability.
>
> *Yell:* Each of the agencies should monitor and assess the implementation of the strategy, and make adjustments as needed (yelling as necessary to ensure adjustments are made).

Juvenile Curfews

A review of the curfew law by the Third District Court of Appeal unanimously indicated that, "Under the Florida and United States Constitutions, children, due to their special nature and vulnerabilities, do not enjoy the same quantum or quality of rights as adults." Shortly thereafter, several Florida cities, including Orlando, Miami Beach, and Miami–Dade, enacted curfew laws to clear the streets of juveniles after 11:00 p.m. Sunday through Thursday and midnight on Friday and Saturday. The curfew mandates that juveniles under 17 and unescorted by an adult are subject to apprehension by the police:

> **F.S. 877.22 Minors prohibited in public places and establishments during certain hours:**
>
> A minor may not be or remain in a public place between the hours of 11:00 p.m. and 5:00 a.m. of the following day, Sunday through Thursday, except in the case of

a legal holiday; and between the hours of 12:01 a.m. and 6:00 a.m. on Saturdays, Sundays, and legal holidays.

A minor who has been suspended or expelled from school may not be or remain in a public place or within 1000 feet of a school during the hours of 9:00 a.m. to 2:00 p.m. during any school day.

A minor who violates this section shall receive a written warning for his/her first violation. A minor who violates this section after having received a prior written warning is guilty of a civil infraction and shall pay a fine of $50 for each violation.

If a minor violates a curfew and is taken into custody, the minor shall be transported immediately to a police station or to a facility operated by a religious, charitable, or civic organization that conducts a curfew program in cooperation with a local law enforcement agency. After recording pertinent information about the minor, the law enforcement agency shall attempt to contact the parent of the minor and, if successful, shall request that the parent take custody of the minor and shall release the minor to the parent. If the law enforcement agency is not able to contact the minor's parent within two hours after the minor is taken into custody, or if the parent refuses to take custody of the minor, the law enforcement agency may transport the minor to his residence or proceed as authorized under Part III of Chapter 39.

Parent's Responsibilities

Under Florida law, parents have the responsibility and legal duty to ensure that their child does not violate the minor-prohibited-in-places law. Parents who knowingly permit their child to violate the law receive a first-offense written warning. If subsequent offenses occur, the parents are guilty of a civil infraction and are subject to a $50 fine for each violation.

Miami–Dade County School System

Miami/Miami–Dade County is the fourth largest school system in the United States. The 312 facilities employ over 50,000 people who serve 369,000 students. About 21,000 teachers instruct students in 16 different languages. The school system also employs a police department of 185. The 27 major public high schools in Miami/Miami–Dade County include grades 10, 11, and 12. The school system manages a budget of approximately $4 billion and is the largest employer in a county of over 2 million residents. A national study conducted by the National Institute of Education in 1976 reported that most school crime is nonviolent. A previous study performed in 1975 and based on the National Crime Survey utilized school victimization data from 26 cities that included Miami. This study also noted the predominance of nonviolent crimes in schools. The data collected for this publication, however, may lead to a different conclusion and suggest a change in direction for crimes committed at school.

MIAMI–DADE COUNTY PUBLIC SCHOOLS
(*n* = 27, 1997/98 ACADEMIC YEAR)

Crime	Frequency
Aggravated battery and assault	145
Simple battery and assault	742
Arson	9
Auto theft	113
Disorderly conduct	120
Homicide	3
Narcotic violations	171
Robbery	129
Sexual assault	13
Weapon violation	117

Currently, Miami–Dade School police are not assigned at elementary schools; however, they do respond to calls for service. Police officers are assigned to middle and high schools. The 1999/2000 juvenile arrest data indicate that 45 arrests were made at elementary schools, 374 at middle schools, and 456 at high schools.

School Crime Prevention

Metal detectors and surveillance cameras are the common types of technologies implemented at schools. An overview of the school systems in Florida (*Miami–Dade School Police Annual Report,* 1997/1998) reveals that 745 metal detectors are used at school entry points (see table). About 99% of those are hand-held, providing mobility for student screening at other school functions. Surveillance cameras are utilized in schools and in some areas on school buses. The 1999/2000 Safe Schools Appropriation Report (FDE, 1999/2000) indicated that over 7000 surveillance cameras are currently in use throughout the state.

METAL DETECTORS BY SCHOOL LEVEL

School Level	Hand-Held	Walk-Through	Total
High schools	275	4	279
Middle schools	319	0	319
Elementary schools	43	0	43
Other	100	4	104

NUMBER OF SURVEILLANCE CAMERAS BY LOCATION

School Level	Cameras
High schools	1992
Middle schools	1401
Elementary schools	1084
School buses	2643
Other	340

Safe Schools Program

Enacted by the Florida Legislature in 1986, the Safe Schools Program provides funding to school districts based on the juvenile crime index. The program restricts funding to three categories: after-school programs, alternative placement, and school safety and security. The funding reports from 1996 to 1999 indicate that alternative placement and after-school programs have received far less attention than school security programs.

In a survey published by the Safe Schools Appropriation Report (1999/2000), statewide school districts were asked to rank the three most critical concerns and safety issues. The three most compelling issues for the responding districts in order of priority were controlling aggressive behavior, disrespect toward teachers, and access control.

JUVENILE JUSTICE SYSTEM IN FLORIDA

Florida is one of a few states with a high juvenile crime rate. It also has the distinction of having the most juveniles in adult prison. In 1978, the legislature gave the prosecutors authority to transfer juveniles directly to the adult court system if they are accused of a felony (Frazier et al., 1996). This would also apply to any juveniles who committed a misdemeanor but had two or more priors, one being a felony (Frazier et al., 1996). During the past 10 years, 6000 to 7000 cases have been transferred annually from juvenile to adult court (Frazier et al., 1996). In 1992/1993, 7353 transfers in Florida occurred, while the nation as a whole transferred 11,800. Many people have argued that the high recidivism rate among juveniles in Florida had to do with this movement.

In 1994, the Florida legislature passed the Juvenile Justice Reform Act. These reforms were passed due to several reasons. First, when the legislature passed the Juvenile Justice Reform Act of 1990, it led to a reduction in the youth population in prison facilities and a growing trend of placement options (Frazier et al., 1996). Little money was available to fund this additional placement, so the lengths of stay in facilities by juveniles were reduced (Frazier et al., 1996). Juvenile arrests rose because many juveniles were in their homes awaiting placement (Frazier et al., 1996). In 1993, a series of tourist killings were committed by juveniles; tourism and Florida's economy were greatly influenced by these killings (Frazier et al., 1996). All of these factors, in combination, led to reforms that stated that punishment and accountability were now part of the juvenile justice system (Frazier et al., 1996).

The 1994 reforms declared three things. First, juveniles 14 or older could be tried as adults, if they had three prior adjudications for felonies, one or more of which involved firearms. Second, youths of any age who were charged with any offense and who had a history of three separate felonies would receive residential commitments. Third, discretion would be given to 14- or 15-year-old youths who were charged with any of the 15 enumerated person and property felony offenses (Frazier et al., 1996). These reforms greatly impacted the juvenile justice system in Florida.

Since 1994, Florida's juvenile crime rate has been on a decline. Between 1994 and 1995, the state had 7760 delinquency referrals per 100,000 juveniles (*Key Juvenile*, 2001). From 1999 to 2000, that figure declined to 6750 delinquency referrals (*Key Juvenile*, 2001). From 1999 to 2000, the 56,447 felony referrals were down 11% from 63,279 felony referrals for 1994 to 1995 (*Key Juvenile*, 2001). Murder/manslaughter was down 25% from 158 for 1994/95 to 118 for 1999/2000 (*Key Juvenile*, 2001). Auto theft was down 35% from 6843 for 1994/95 to 4447 for 1999/2000 (*Key Juvenile*, 2001). Burglary was down 16% from 20,270 for 1994/95 to 16,941 for 1999/2000 (*Key Juvenile*, 2001). However, aggravated assaults and battery were up 25% from 9075 for 1994/95 to 11,342 for 1999/2000 (*Key Juvenile*, 2001). Drug arrests have also skyrocketed. During the 1990s, there was a 229% increase in drug offenses (*Key Juvenile*, 2001).

Juveniles being tried as adults are on a decline, from 5350 for 1995/96 to 3297 for 1999/2000 (*Key Juvenile*, 2001). Yet, Florida still tries more juveniles as adults than any other state (*Key Juvenile*, 2001). Of all juvenile offenders, 14% are labeled as chronic offenders; chronic offenders usually commit six or more delinquent crimes in a 2-year period (*Key Juvenile*, 2001). Recidivism rates have also been declining; 58% of juveniles in 1998 stayed out of trouble for at least a year, as opposed to 54% in 1996 (*Key Juvenile*, 2001). Approximately 58% of juveniles do not go into the juvenile system for a second time (*Key Juvenile*, 2001).

It appears as though the juvenile system in Florida has been successful in recent years. The crime rate, in almost every category, has been dropping. The rate of juveniles being tried as adults has also been declining.

Police and the Juvenile Offender

The 1968 Uniform Juvenile Court Act provides guidelines for police agencies to develop policies for dealing with juveniles. According to the Act:

> A child taken into custody shall not be detained or placed in shelter care prior to the hearing on the petition unless his or her detention of care is required to protect the person or property of others or of the child or because the child may abscond or be removed from the jurisdiction of the court or because he or she has no parent, guardian, or custodian or other person able to provide supervision and care for him or her and returning the child to the court when required, or an order for his or her detention or shelter care has been made by the court pursuant to this act.

The Juvenile System

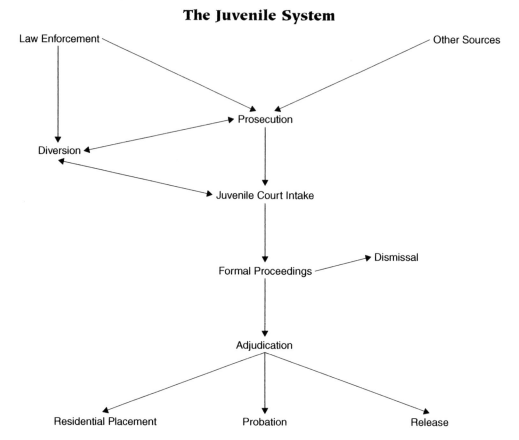

(*Source: Juvenile Offenders National Report 2001.* Washington, D.C.: National Center for Juvenile Justice.)

Taking a Juvenile into Custody

A juvenile may be taken into custody by the police under the following circumstances:

> Pursuant to an order of the circuit court:
>> For failure to appear at court after being properly noticed; or
>> For a delinquent act or violation of law pursuant to a lawful arrest. Should this act committed by a juvenile be considered a felony if committed by an adult, the police shall immediately notify the district school superintendent. The police should also attempt to notify the parent or legal custodian of the child. The law clearly indicates that a child taken into custody is not an arrest except for the purpose of obtaining any evidence in conjunction with the act.

Unless otherwise ordered by the court, a child taken into custody is to be released as soon as reasonably possible. The probable cause affidavit is forwarded to the juvenile court.

Fingerprinting and Photographing Juveniles

A child who is apprehended for an act that would be considered a felony or a misdemeanor by an adult can be fingerprinted. A law enforcement agency may fingerprint and photograph a child taken into custody upon probable cause that the child has committed any other violation of the law. All fingerprints and photographs are required to be kept in a separate file clearly marked as "juvenile confidential."

Temporary Detention of a Juvenile

Temporary detention is conducted by an intake counselor or case manager who reviews the facts and probable cause affidavit. This counselor makes the decision as to whether or not the juvenile is placed in secure detention. Under no circumstances does the counselor, the police, or the state attorney authorize detention of a juvenile in a facility intended for the detention of adults.

Adjudication Hearing

An adjudication hearing is held as soon as possible after the alleged offense. The court does not find guilt or innocence during this procedure; it only determines whether or not a child is delinquent. However, this procedure can be postponed for purpose of investigation, discovery, and other matters related to the violation. For children who are charged with an offense that, if committed by an adult, would be punishable by death or life imprisonment, the adjudication hearing is required to be postponed for 21 days unless the state's attorney office notifies the court that it does not intend to present the case to the grand jury.

Disposition Hearing

Once a child has been found to have committed a delinquent act and adjudicated a delinquent, the court determines the disposition of the matter in terms of imposing sanctions or rehabilitation programs. In making its determination, the court shall consider the child's entire assessment and predisposition report for purposes of final disposition. Before final disposition, the court is required to:

1. State clearly, using common terminology, the purpose of the hearing and the rights of persons present.

2. Discuss with the child his or her compliance with any home release plan or any other plan imposed since the offense.

3. Discuss with the child his or her feelings about the offense and the harm to victims.

4. Give all parties present an opportunity to comment on the issue of disposition and suggestions for rehabilitation.

Options of the Court

As a result of the disposition hearing and its procedures, some of the options available to the court in terms of sanctions and rehabilitation programs are as follows:

- The court can place the child in a community control program, in the child's own home, in the home of one of the child's relatives, or in any other location found suitable by the court. A community control program must include a penalty such as a monetary or in-kind restitution, community service, curfew, revocation or suspension of driving privileges, or other appropriate nonresidential punishment. Additionally, the community control program must also include a rehabilitative component such as participation in a substance-abuse treatment program, if applicable, or in an education program.

- The court may commit the child to a licensed child-care agency but may not commit the child to a jail or facility used primarily as a detention center or shelter.

- The court may commit the child into the active control of the Department of Juvenile Justice for purpose of custody, care, training, drug-testing monitoring, treatment, and furlough into the community.

- The court may revoke or suspend the driver's license of the child.

- The court may require the child, and/or the child's parent or guardian, if appropriate, to perform community service in a public service program.

- The court may commit the child to the Department of Juvenile Justice for placement in a program or facility for serious or habitual offenders.

Waiver Hearing

Within 7 days of the offense, the state's attorney office may file a motion requesting the court to transfer the child for criminal prosecution. The court shall conduct a hearing on all transfer requests for the purpose of determining the purpose of transfer. The court:

1. Evaluates the seriousness of the offense.

2. Determines the alleged offense as a crime against person or property.

3. Scrutinizes the strength of probable cause.

4. Assesses the sophistication and maturity of the child.

5. Reviews the criminal history of the child.

6. Evaluates reasonableness of rehabilitation.

7. Determines the possibility of threat to public safety.

Juveniles Transferred as Adults

Once a child has been transferred for criminal prosecution, the juvenile is entitled to every right afforded to an adult. Effective January 1, 1995, a juvenile who is charged with an offense of arson, sexual battery, robbery, kidnapping, aggravated assault, stalking, child abuse, murder, manslaughter, bombing, armed burglary, or using a weapon during the commission of a felony is subject to criminal adult court.

Florida Department of Juvenile Justice

The Juvenile Justice Act of 1994 created the Florida Department of Juvenile Justice. It relieved the Department of Health and Rehabilitative Services of the responsibility and oversight of the juvenile justice services. The mission of the Department of Juvenile Justice is to provide a full range of programs and services to prevent and reduce juvenile delinquency in partnership with families, schools, communities, and law enforcement agencies. The Florida Department of Juvenile Justice is responsible for planning and managing all programs and services related to ungovernable truants, runaways, early intervention and diversion, case management, detention, community-based programs, juvenile justice facilities, and prevention programs.

The Grand Jury Report

The Grand Jury Report of 1995 on the juvenile justice system reported that Miami–Dade County had the highest juvenile offense problem in the state and it predicted a tidal wave of future juvenile crime if reforms were not enacted. The report criticized the dilapidated and completely insufficient facilities provided for the juvenile courts. Cases were cited that clearly indicated the juveniles charged with serious felonies had little chance of punishment or respect for the system. The grand jury recommended that future considerations involve a sentencing guideline similar to that of adult court and called for a complete revision of the entire system.

The call for juvenile justice reform has been echoed by Rutter (1980) and Wilson and Hernstein (1985), and Regnery (1985), who suggested that:

> Criminals should be treated as criminals. ... Society may wish to be lenient with first offenders, particularly for lesser crimes, but there is no reason that society should be more lenient with a 16-year-old first offender than a 30-year-old first offender. Anyone familiar with the nature of juvenile crime will not make the argument that juvenile crimes differ in their magnitude or brutality from adult crimes; in many cases, the reverse is true. So, the current approach which makes a radical distinction between criminals under 18 and those over 18 is often counterproductive.

The Office of Youthful Offenders

The Office of Youthful Offenders was established in 1994. Its mission is to encourage correction and the successful return to society of the youthful offender. While in state prison, offenders should be provided with vocational, educational, counseling, or public service opportunities. The separate facilities will prevent association with older, more experienced criminals during the term of their confinement.

The Office of Youthful Offenders is responsible for the following:

- basic training facilities in Sumter County for first time offenders

- specialized programming for over 2500 inmates

- classification of activities and inmates

- coordination of all academic and vocational programs

- controlling, transferring, and placing inmates

- coordination of special needs and programs

Who Is Sentenced as a Youthful Offender

According to F.S. 958.04, those who commit a crime prior to their 21st birthday could be categorized as youthful offenders. The Department of Corrections may classify an inmate as a youthful offender if the inmate is:

- age 24 or under with a sentence of 10 years or less

- 19 or under with more than a sentence of 10 years

- not a capital or life felon

- a youthful offender 14 to 18 years old (such an inmate must be kept separate from youthful offenders 19 to 24 years old)

STATE OF FLORIDA YOUTHFUL OFFENDERS (1995)

Location	Age Range	Security Level	Population
Indian River	18 and under	Medium/minimum	243
Hillsborough	18 and under	High/medium/minimum	307
Lancaster CI	19–24	Medium/minimum	599
Lancaster WC	19–24	Medium/minimum	254
Brevard	19–24	High/medium/minimum	945
Sumter (boot camp)	24 and under	Medium/minimum	76
Florida (female)	24 and under	High/medium/minimum	55
Reception centers	24 and under	High/medium/minimum	525
Community centers	24 and under	Minimum	211
Department of Juvenile Justice	24 and under	Minimum	4

Juvenile Boot Camps

Georgia and Oklahoma were the first states to put the concept of boot camps into practice in 1983 (Weis et al., 1996). Florida's first boot camp opened in Manatee County in 1993. The concept has spread throughout the state, with another ten or so juvenile boot camps being added. These facilities attempt to provide rehabilitation through discipline, regimentation, physical fitness, counseling, and education. The atmosphere reflects a strict military entrance training program.

A Typical Day in Boot Camp

The Volusia juvenile boot camp office describes a typical day of incarceration:

> All inmates are awakened at 5:00 a.m. The morning meal is served from 5:30 a.m. to 6:00 a.m. Inmates spend about one hour cleaning the housing facility and preparing for inspections. By early morning the physical training has started which includes running, calisthenics, an obstacle course, and other demanding physical activities. The remainder of the morning is consumed by classroom education. After the 30-minute lunch break, the inmates return to the classroom for another two hours. The afternoon education training is followed by a two-hour counseling session. The afternoon continues with regimented precision drilling until the evening meal is served at 5:30 p.m. The next three hours are depleted with study sessions, followed by the washing and ironing of uniforms. All inmates are secured prior to the mandatory 9:00 p.m. lights out. The exact same routine starts at 5:00 a.m. the next morning.

The Projected Success of Boot Camps

If history is an indication of the success of shock-related programs for the correction of juvenile delinquency, then failure may be likely. In the early 1970s, the shock program Scared Straight was initiated in the maximum security correction facility in Rahway, New Jersey. The program allowed juveniles with behavioral problems to visit the prison and hear about the realities of prison life from hardened convicts. This program, despite its national attention, performed poorly in terms of delinquency prevention. The value of the shock objective of boot camp programs has also come under serious fire. Nevertheless, advocates continue to defend the program as an effective incarceration and rehabilitation method for juveniles.

CONCLUSION

Prior to the 20th century, there was little differentiation in the treatment between juveniles and adults within the criminal justice system. Currently, Florida law defines a juvenile as a person under the age of 18. The Florida Department of Corrections may classify an inmate as a youthful offender if he or she is 24 years of age or younger with a 10-year or less sentence or is 19 years of age or younger with more than a 10-year sentence. Additionally, the Florida Department of Corrections may not classify a capital or life felon as a youthful offender, and all juveniles ages 14 to 18 must be kept separate from 19- to 24-year-old offenders.

With the projected doubling of violent crimes committed by juveniles, the criminal justice system must address how to treat child offenders who commit adult crimes, how to rehabilitate them, and how to protect society, as well as to determine the cause of increases in these crimes.

Several cities within Florida have enacted curfew laws that prohibit juveniles under the age of 17 and unescorted by an adult from being on the streets after 11:00 p.m. Sunday through Thursday and after midnight on Friday and Saturday.

Boot camp in Florida has become a popular method to rehabilitate the juvenile offender. The concept of boot camps has been in practice since as early as 1983 in Georgia and Oklahoma. Florida's first boot camp opened in 1993 in Manatee County. Even with this type of rehabilitation being employed in the State of Florida, 3129 youthful offenders were in Florida's correctional facilities in 1995.

DISCUSSION QUESTIONS

1. Identify methods of addressing the juvenile delinquency problem in the State of Florida.

2. Discuss Florida's juvenile gangs and the acronym IDENTIFY.

3. Discuss Florida's boot camp system and its potential for success.

4. Discuss the process of adjudicating a child as a delinquent or applying a waiver as an adult.

5. Discuss the disposition options of the court.

REFERENCES

Department of Police. 1986. *Crime Reports*. Miami, Fla.: Dade County School Board.

FDE. 1999/2000. *Safe Schools Appropriation Report*. Tallahassee, Fla.: State of Florida.

Florida Criminal Law and Motor Vehicle Handbook. 1996. Longwood, Fla.: Gould Publications.

Frazier, C. et al. 1996. *Journal of Research in Crime and Delinquency*, 42: 171–191.

Key Juvenile Crime Trends and Conditions. 2001. Tallahassee, Fla.: Office of Technology, State of Florida.

Kids Count Data Book. 1995. Baltimore, Md.: The Casey Foundation.

Miami–Dade School Police Annual Report. 1997/1998. Miami–Dade County, Fla.

National Advisory Committee on Criminal Justice Standards and Goals. 1976. *Juvenile Justice and Delinquency Prevention*. Washington, D.C.: Law Enforcement Assistance Administration.

Regnery, A. S. 1985. Getting away with murder. *Police Review*, 34: 1–4.

Rutter, M. 1980. *Changing Youth in a Changing Society*. Cambridge, Mass.: Harvard University Press.

Thompson, W. E. and J. E. Bynum. 1991. *Juvenile Delinquency: Classic and Contemporary Readings*. Boston, Mass.: Allyn & Bacon.

U.S. Department of Justice. 1995. Office of Juvenile Justice and Delinquency Prevention, U.S. Bureau of Census. Washington, D.C.: U.S. Government Printing Office.

Wilson, J. and Hernstein, R. 1985. *Crime and Human Nature*. New York: Simon & Schuster.

Consolidation, Productivity, and Privatization as Future Considerations for Law Enforcement

CHAPTER OVERVIEW

Law enforcement and the criminal justice system must look for new approaches to solving problems. Reduced resources, increased demand for services, population growth, and fragmentation of police services contribute to the growing need for a new direction for the law enforcement community and society. The size, structure, and productivity of law enforcement and resources available in various communities pose varying problems that possibly could be solved through consolidation of efforts, coordination of personnel, and integration of financial and nonfinancial resources. This chapter looks at the various issues that can be addressed, why we are forced to confront them, and how we can position ourselves for the future.

THE ISSUE OF POLICE CONSOLIDATION

Police Management

The essence of police management is the administration of the process by which resources are allocated to a police service (Gourley, 1967). This definition is applicable to all law enforcement functions regardless of the number of personnel. Police management at every level requires planning, organizing, leading, and utilizing finances and equipment to attain a set of predetermined goals.

The effectiveness of police agencies has been questioned (Kelling et al., 1974), and law enforcement services are being held to the same standards of accountability as other municipal services (Cuniff, 1984; Ostrom et al., 1977). This trend of greater accountability is important in Florida, as municipal resources are becoming more constrained and police agencies are competing with other local agencies for limited financial resources.

The Problem in Florida

Currently, many Florida municipalities, cities, and towns are experiencing financial pressures due to increased demands from citizens, motivated primarily by rising taxes, expansion of the population, and fragmentation of governmental services (Wiatrowski, 1984). Some police departments in Florida are facing serious problems in terms of attempting to deliver effective police services with fewer financial resources. This type of problem appears to be escalating throughout the state, and in the short run police administrators are being put in the difficult position of meeting demands of crime control with diminished means. The following realities indicate that the period of police autonomy could be in jeopardy:

- Florida citizens demanding economy in local government
- local budgets dealing with inflation and other pressures
- decreasing budget resources
- increasing populations
- increasing demands on police for additional services
- increasing demands for police visibility
- citizen demands for crime control and reduction
- citizen demands for proper investigations and prosecution
- citizen involvement with police administration, advisory groups, and community interest groups
- citizen demands for police to deal with social issues, such as street and homeless people

The issue for Florida police administrators is whether local resources are distributed in a manner consistent with expectations of the public. The police in Florida appear to be facing budgetary reductions coupled with increased citizen demands for service. Police administrators will be forced to respond with innovative, practical methods for delivery of police services.

The Status of Florida Police

Florida continues to have one of the most rapidly growing populations in the United States. In addition to this growth in citizens, the number of visitors is estimated to be over 35 million each year (*Florida Statistical Abstract*, 1995). While more police have been provided to respond to the increase, the crime problem remains at the forefront of public attention. The approximately 340 police agencies in the State of Florida frequently overlap in their jurisdictions and in many instances duplicate investigations, recordkeeping, reporting, and related police services. This has long been recognized as a source of inefficiency of the police (Angell et al., 1974). Three major problems have emerged among the abundant number of police agencies:

- coordination of police efforts
- communication among police departments
- cooperation among police departments

The irregular configuration of jurisdictional lines, the growing population, increasing number of tourists, and the complexity and sophistication of modern criminal behavior indicate a need for an alternative to the current system of police service delivery.

Consolidation in Criminal Justice

Future consolidation of some police departments may be necessary for the provision of an adequate level of service. The concept of consolidation in the Florida criminal justice system has been applied successfully in several areas. In 1972, revision of the judicial article of the state constitution consolidated the Florida court system and eliminated all local jurisdictional courts. In some cases, the fragmented management of municipal courts resulted in incompetent judges and speed-trap-reputation communities. The correctional system also has experienced reform through consolidating local jails with the county and state prison systems. Many areas found that they could not afford dispatching mobile units from independent jurisdictions, so dispatching was consolidated to a regional level, with each participating jurisdiction contributing funds to support the consolidated effort. Due to the high cost of training, many police jurisdictions have consolidated their basic training to a centralized facility. In the near future, police administrators may be faced with a difficult decision in choosing a route to deliver proper police services. The decision may be complicated by the advent of political realities that oppose any form of centralization of police. Some political leaders do not endorse the loss of control, regardless of its benefits (Ferrell and Foster, 1982). In maintaining their independence, police have responded to budget restrictions in numerous ways: freezing hiring, foregoing pay increases, creating retirement incentives, reducing or freezing overtime, and eliminating some specialized units. These pressures have forced police administrators to reexamine the manner in which police services are delivered. Ironically, some local jurisdictions not only may be resistant to consolidation but may also be directed toward further decentralization. Declaring independence from county jurisdiction and creating a small area with its own police agency appears to be preferred by some communities. Many small jurisdictions in South Florida have already attempted to gain independence from county government (e.g., Key Biscayne and Aventura). The well-intended community motives for such action may have severe financial and practical complications in the future.

The History of Fragmented Police Departments

The traditional, small Florida police agency may not be able to adjust to the expanding populations and new forms of criminal behavior. These contemporary trends are taxing the capabilities of small police agencies. As the population continues to grow significantly in Florida, the municipal boundaries may become barriers to the solution of crime and community problems. Many aspects of the crime problem reach beyond political boundaries. Most small police departments have mounted only a limited response to the crime problem. The following deficiencies have emerged for small agencies as they deal with major crimes:

- crime laboratories

- aircraft support

- mobile crime scene investigation support

- computerized reporting and recordkeeping

- mobile blood alcohol testing units

- fatality accident investigation units

- narcotic criminal investigation and tracking

- felony domestic violence investigations

- crime analysis

- centralized communication

At best, the small independent police department may become a luxury that communities may not be able to afford. The issue of jurisdictional lines becomes important to citizens who are victimized on or near community boundaries. The exact scene of the crime will determine the police agency responsible for reporting and the subsequent investigation. Occasionally, disputes can emerge between police agencies over jurisdictions.

The Cost of Police

People demand and expect high levels of police performance without committing to financially supporting such law enforcement service. One of the major components of the police budget is the cost of personnel. Approximately 75% of most law enforcement budgets is designated for wages and salaries. Cuniff (1984) noted that it costs almost $125,000 to maintain one police officer on patrol on a 24-hour basis. The cost of the patrol vehicle and its maintenance is less than 20% of this total figure.

Some Advantage in Size

One major benefit of a large police agency is the opportunity for division of labor. Such agencies have ample opportunities for specialization of their personnel. It has been suggested that an officer who has received additional training in homicide investigation, traffic accident reconstruction, or other technical crime investigation could be more productive and solve more cases quickly and at a lower cost. This type of specialization simply exceeds the ability of small independent police departments. The small-police-agency officer may consume an overwhelming amount of hours on an investigation that a highly trained officer could resolve expeditiously.

Criminal Mobility

Criminals and crime patterns are not restricted to jurisdictional boundaries. The numerous variables that may affect a criminal's target selection or identification of opportunity will not be reiterated here; however, research has demonstrated that criminals often do cross jurisdictional lines. The Normandeau (1968) study of robberies in Philadelphia, Pennsylvania, showed that the mean travel distance from place of residence to place of robbery was 1.57 miles. The Capone and Nichols (1976) study of robbery in Miami, Florida, reported that 41% of all armed robbers resided more than 3 miles from their victims. The Pope (1980) study of burglary in California found that more than 50% of all burglars live in excess of 1 mile from the crime scene. These findings are supported by the Florida Department of Law Enforcement *Annual Report,* which indicates that, of the total arrests reported by municipal law enforcement agencies, about 40% of the perpetrators resided outside the jurisdiction of the arresting agency. This may suggest that criminals crossing jurisdictional lines is a significant problem for smaller jurisdictions.

Public Expectations

For some, recent crime trends, victimization rates, and fear of crime perceptions have been the basis for questioning the effectiveness of law enforcement in the State of Florida. Due to contained municipal resources, local police departments must compete with other local government departments for funding. Citizens and interest groups are demanding that law enforcement develop accountability standards comparable with other municipal services. The traditionally high degree of autonomy enjoyed among local police has transformed into community demands for economy, budgetary restrictions, increased service, and crime control.

Problems of Multiple Jurisdictions

The traditional small police agency may not be able to adjust to the expanding population, criminal activity, and emergency circumstances in the multiculture communities of Florida. Municipal boundaries may soon become barriers to providing solutions to crimes and other problems. Most municipal police agencies do not have the financial resources to operate a crime laboratory or utilize a mobile crime lab at major crime scenes, to have complicated computerized records system, to investigate the transient nature of narcotic offenses, or to obtain helicopter or aircraft support, and they may not have the training or experience to deal with major emergency events.

Arguments for Consolidation of Police

Consolidation of police services for Florida will potentially provide more public service at a lower cost per unit. Small police agencies are expensive to operate. Hillman and Peterson (1980) concluded that consolidation of police services can reduce costs and improve the delivery of police service. The issue of determining who will assume control after consolidation is a consistent problem that was addressed in California when five small agencies consolidated into one to overcome a number of law enforcement obstacles that existed under the separate agency approach. In this case, existing chiefs of police realigned into a board of directors system of supervision.

Arguments against Police Consolidation

The foundation for the consolidation of police services is that the delivery of service will be more effective and will be conducted at a lower cost. In contrast, several issues can be identified in opposition of police consolidation:

- Consolidated police reduce close contact between law enforcement officers and the community.

- Police officers are less likely to be familiar with the criminal element or problems in the community.

- A chief of police not responsible to local citizens loses his authority.

Future Issues To Be Studied

A significant issue for the future is whether consolidation is a viable response to the crime problems in Florida. Several studies (Vardalis, 1985) indicate that as police agencies increase in size the cost of providing police services declines. The declining curve results from extensive training, specialization, and more effective utilization of police personnel and resources. The challenge confronting the police administrators and political leaders is the exploration and careful evaluation of alternatives to traditional independent policing that provide citizens with efficient and cost-effective police services.

The contemporary citizen's approach to government appears to demand economy in its operations, including law enforcement departments. Inflationary pressures and other strains on the budget require law enforcement officials to examine other options of the delivery of service to the public. Most research suggests that centralization of small agencies provides the public with better police service at a lower cost of operation. The consolidation model of police services in Florida is a possible solution to the problems the state faces.

THE ISSUE OF POLICE PRODUCTIVITY

Accountability

Another issue for future consideration is law enforcement accountability and determining productivity. Traditionally, the police, as a social organization, have enjoyed a high degree of autonomy. The development of the professional model of policing removed the police from the political process and limited the potential for corruption. The concept of public trust is clearly associated with accountability. The professional model has classified the police product into law enforcement activities. The funding of agencies is also closely affiliated with productivity; therefore, police have created numerous methods for logging, counting, analyzing, and quantifying police work. Police administrators have traditionally responded to this concept by developing an organizational structure that provides a military model with successive levels of supervision.

The Police Product

The professional model defines the product of the police in terms of arrests (both misdemeanor and felony), traffic citations, and crime data. O'Brien (1985) reported that in many cases funding is directly related to the appropriate level of productivity. To a substantial degree, in the professional approach, many police supervisors project a philosophy that encourages tangible enforcement as documentation for accountability. In some cases, patrol officers at the completion of a shift who are devoid of arrest reports or traffic tickets may have great difficulty accounting for their time. In addition to law enforcement activity, the number of calls for service is utilized as a police product. The consequence of counting calls for service could result in one disturbance requiring numerous returns by the police because the issue of productivity encourages officers to clear a call quickly with little or no immediate resolution of the problem. Police work involves more than dealing with crime, and police officers are confronted with many forms of behavior that are not defined as criminal or require law enforcement (Goldstein, 1990). This traditional method of counting arrests, tickets, and calls for service may have, in many cases, fueled the adversarial relationship between the police and the community.

New Roles for the Police Officer

The future role of the police officer may be driven by a patrol emphasis on crime prevention, community problem solving, and order maintenance. It will be necessary for police officers to develop a plan to conceptualize short, medium, and long-range goals. Short- and medium-range goals target specific problems in the community, while medium- and long-range goals deal with the development of community resources. Some police agencies have revised their method of police responsibility by creating a means to recognize officers who excel in solving disputes, providing guidance for crime prevention, and promoting general order maintenance. The police as problem solvers tend to view arrest as only one of the many options available.

Reorientation for Police

Evidence of the inability of the police to utilize the professional model successfully to suppress and control crime is fairly conclusive (Packer, 1988). New strategies for police, including community policing, have emerged as viable alternatives for the method in which police services are delivered. An approach of problem resolution and proactive crime tactics that deal with a wide spectrum of public concerns is a possible direction for future policing. The process of developing accountability systems for contemporary police is predicated on the development of an overall strategy for what the police agency is attempting to accomplish. The shift from reactionary policing to problem-solving policing may be in conflict with the traditional method of measurement of productivity; therefore, new methods of determining the police product and procedure for accountability must be developed.

THE ISSUE OF PRIVATE POLICE

The User-Fee Concept

The three components of the concept of private police are:

1. *Private component of public police*—Non-sworn personnel perform a traditional task of the public police.

2. *Off-duty police as security*—Sworn police officers are employed by a private party to perform a security role.

3. *Public police privatized*—Public police are offered to the public under the user-fee concept.

Exclusion and *joint consumption* are terms used to categorize various services under the user-fee concept. Generally, a service that is consumed by a few who pay for it is considered a private good; however, some goods that are consumed collectively (e.g., water and electricity) may still be charged to an individual in proportion to use (Savas, 1982). Police service can be regarded in a similar manner. Service is the commodity of the police, and the distribution of such service is consumed collectively; however, those who desire additional service should pay in proportion to that use. In the user-fee police service model, the basic police service is provided via taxes to the general population; consumers who require additional services pay additional fees. Other approaches with less direct compensation to the officer have included private businesses supplementing certain expenses of walking or equestrian police. Examples of this type of privatization are rapidly developing in many cities, including Oakland, California, where a group of business persons who wanted to attract more customers to the downtown shopping area entered into an agreement to pay the city for additional patrols (Steward, 1985). Additionally, the Montclair Plaza shopping center in Montclair, California, entered into a contract with the city to fund 50%

of salary and benefits of all officers assigned to the mall beat (Moulton, 1983). Other cities have entered into similar agreements, applying the user-fee concept; this model becomes more defensible when financial benefit is realized by consuming more than the basic police service. The future of this concept in Florida may require beach enthusiasts to pay additional fees to support police beach patrol, which can be argued on the grounds that such a patrol benefits only those who frequent the beach.

Off-Duty Police as Security

In Florida and other areas throughout the United States, a fundamental shift in the method of the delivery of security service is emerging. The method has been identified as consumer-controlled or client-directed public police employed with private contracts. Typically, police officers who engage in off-duty employment are assigned to specific geographical areas of neighborhoods or locations with specific tasks.

The private employment of public police operates as one of three basic models by which compensation for off-duty hours is obtained. Reiss (1991) has identified three management models of private employment of public police:

1. The *officer contract model* allows for each officer to locate and negotiate tasks, hours, and pay.

2. The *union brokerage model* has the police union finding and distributing off-duty work.

3. The *department contract model* permits the police department to control and assign extra employment.

Many police departments employ somewhat different but similar models or a variation that may incorporate two or more models.

The style of off-duty employment varies throughout the state. Most officers in South Florida utilize a system similar to the contract model to obtain secondary employment; however, the agency does maintain some degree of control over extra employment by requiring the officer to submit an application for off-duty employment. The courts have supported the authority of police agencies to place limits on off-duty work (*Cox v. McNamara*, 1972; *Brenckle v. Township of Shaler*, 1972). Most police departments have general orders regulating extra employment for police personnel.

The impact of private employment of public police is twofold. First, the large number of off-duty uniform police can have a significant influence on the regular patrol shift, in terms of handling some services that normally would require a duty officer. Second, such officers impact the proactive model of policing by increasing the visibility of uniformed police throughout the city. Police present the same law enforcement image, regardless of whether they are paid by public taxes or private funds.

The consumer-controlled off-duty employment of police is a proactive tactic that seems to be well received by citizens in the South Florida area. The trend of utilizing supplemental police for neighborhoods, subdivisions, malls, and other establishments appears to be most common in communities that can afford more police service than the city is currently providing. Areas of affluent citizens that have identifiable boundaries are especially receptive to having a police officer confined to a designated area. Newman's (1972) classical defensible-space theory identified those numerous environmental factors and conditions that reduce criminal opportunity. The addition of a uniformed police officer to the familiar factors identified in Newman's theory may significantly decrease the probability of crime occurrence. With the continuous, reliable assignment of police to a certain neighborhood, consensual rules for public behavior are enforced by members of that community.

Private Component of Public Police

Over the last decade, trends in public law enforcement have dictated that a significant number of public police assignments be distributed to the private sector. The reclassification of numerous tasks that have been historically held by police officers continues to occur. This concept has changed the entire relationship between the public and private sector. Examples include private dispatch centers, records divisions, and crime analyses. Consequently, the private sector has significantly reduced the number of long-established police assignments. Currently, Miami–Dade County has contracted with a private security company to provide safety at the downtown courthouse and other selected public buildings. Many police departments now employ non-sworn personnel, commonly referred to as community service aides or PR public service aides, to respond to public requests regarding non-criminal matters.

The Future of Privatizing Florida

There appears to be little question that privatizing areas within the Florida criminal justice system will have a major role in the future. Several county sheriffs are seeking proposals from private security companies to provide relief to the overcrowded jails. The court system is investigating the use of private security within the judicial system. The persuasiveness of furnishing private security and supplementing personnel within the criminal justice system is significant. The 1990 Hallcrest II report (Cunningham et al., 1990) indicated that the total U.S. employment of personnel in private security functions was 1,493,000; however, that figure was projected to grow to 1,900,000 by the year 2005.

CONCLUSION

Some police departments in Florida are facing serious problems in terms of attempting to deliver effective police services with fewer financial resources. This situation may jeopardize police autonomy and force police administrators to respond with innovative, practical methods to deliver police services. Overlapping jurisdictions of the approximately 340 police agencies in the State of Florida result in duplication in investigations, recordkeeping, reporting, and related police services; inefficient police systems; a lack of coordination of police efforts, communication among police departments, and cooperation among police. Consolidation of police service may be necessary to maintain the adequate level of service the community demands.

Consolidation of services has been attempted in other public areas, such as the Florida court system, which eliminated all local jurisdictional courts and consolidated local jails into the county and state prison systems. The time may have come for law enforcement to closely examine the issue of consolidation. Naturally, there are advantages and disadvantages to this issue. Supporters of consolidation argue that it will provide more public service at a lower cost per unit. The quality of service could increase due to efficient, consolidated resources. On the other hand, opponents contend that police consolidation will reduce close contact between law enforcement officers and the community, police will be less familiar with the criminal element or problems of a community, and the local chief of police will lose authority while still being held responsible to local citizens.

Another issue to be addressed in the future is that of privatizing police service through non-sworn personnel performing traditional tasks of public police, using off-duty police as security, and privatizing public police. A user-fee concept could be applied to provide individual police service not absorbed collectively by the general public. Several models of managing off-duty police have been identified for the private employment of public police: the officer contract model, the union brokerage model, and the department contract model.

DISCUSSION QUESTIONS

1. Discuss how financial limitations can affect police service delivery.

2. Discuss the advantages and disadvantages of consolidation.

3. What is the police product under the professional model?

4. Identify the three management models of off-duty employment.

5. Discuss the future of privatization in criminal justice.

REFERENCES

Angell, J. E., S. A. Egger, and F. Hagedorn. 1974. *Police Consolidation Project: Staff Report.* Portland, OR: Police Consolidation Project.

Brenckle v. Township of Shaler. 1972. 28 A.2d, 970 (PA).

Capone, D. C. and W. W. Nichols, Jr. 1976. Urban structure and criminal mobility. *American Behavorial Scientist*, 20(2).

Cox v. McNamara. 1972. 493 P. 2nd, 54 (Ore).

Cuniff, M. 1984. *Beyond Crime: Law Enforcement Operational and Cost Data.* Washington, D.C.: National Association of Criminal Justice Planners.

Cunningham, W. C., J. J. Strauchs, and C. W. VanMeter. 1990. *Private Security Trends 1970–2000 (The Hallcrest Report II).* Stoneham, MA: Butterworth-Heinemann.

Ferrell, T. and B. Foster. 1982. Obstacles to police consolidation. *Journal of Police Science and Administration*, 10(1).

Florida Statistical Abstract. 1995. Gainesville, FL: University of Florida.

Goldstein, H. 1990. *Problem-Oriented Policing.* New York: McGraw-Hill.

Gourley, G. D. 1967. *Effective Police Organization and Management: State Police Systems.* Long Beach, CA: California State College.

Hillman, M. and D. Peterson. 1980. Guide to cooperative law enforcement. *Journal of South Dakota Criminal Justice.* U.S. Department of Law Enforcement Assistance Administration.

Kelling, G. et al. 1974. *The Kansas City Preventive Patrol Experiment.* Washington, D.C.: The Police Foundation.

Moulton, R. 1983. Police contract service for shopping mall security. *Police Chief.*

Newman, O. 1972. *Defensible Space.* New York: Macmillan.

Normandeau, A. 1968. Trends and Patterns in the Crime of Robbery, Ph.D. dissertation. Philadelphia, PA: University of Pennsylvania.

O'Brien, R. M. 1985. *Crime and Victimization Data.* Beverly Hills, CA: Sage Publishing.

Packer, H. L. 1988. *The Limits of the Criminal Sanction.* Palo Alto, CA: Stanford University Press.

Pope, C. E. 1980. Patterns in burglary: an empirical examination of offense and offender characteristics. *Journal of Criminal Justice,* 8(1).

Reiss, A. J. 1991. *Private Employment of Public Police.* Washington, D.C.: National Institute of Justice, U.S. Department of Justice.

Savas, E. S. 1982. *Privatizing the Public Sector.* Chatham, NJ: Chatham House Press.

Steward, J. 1985. Public safety and private police. *Public Administration Review*, November.

Vardalis, J. J. 1985. Unpublished manuscript. Miami, FL: Department of Criminal Justice, Florida International University.

Wiatrowski, M. 1984. *Tax Limitation Amendments and Law Enforcement* (unpublished manuscript). Boca Raton, FL: Florida Atlantic University.